T0195812

One Man's Search for God

A Retrospective On Divine Providence

An Autobiography by
Rex L. Sample

WESTBOW
PRESS°
A DIVISION OF THOMAS NELSON
& ZONDERVAN

WestBow Press books may be ordered through booksellers or by contacting:

WestBow Press
A Division of Thomas Nelson & Zondervan
1663 Liberty Drive
Bloomington, IN 47403
www.westbowpress.com
1 (866) 928-1240

ISBN: 978-1-9736-7296-8 (sc)
ISBN: 978-1-9736-7370-5 (hc)
ISBN: 978-1-9736-7297-5 (e)

Print information available on the last page.

WestBow Press rev. date: 9/4/2019

This book is dedicated to the memory of Reverend Walter Jewett, who played such a significant role in my life story.

Contents

Preface ix

1 Remembering My Ancestors.................................. 1

2 My Early Years.. 13

3 An Awakening... 49

4 My High School Years 53

5 So This Is College 67

6 Look Before You Leap 91

7 Learning to Swim..121

8 Becoming an Entrepreneur.................................131

9 Following My Heart..151

10 When Family Comes First 161

11 Remember You Are an Entreprenuer 173

12 Returning to My Hearts Desire 185

13 A Retrospective on Divine Providence...............195

14 Finding Your Way to the Father............................ 209

Preface

IT WAS A BEAUTIFUL SUNDAY MORNING IN OUR comfortable retirement cottage in Camp Verde, Arizona. My daughter, Terri, was here visiting from Phoenix. It has been 4 years since I retired as Pastor from Munds Park Community Church in Munds Park, Arizona, and now at age 85 some pressing health issues have prompted me to think about what God would want me to do with the last chapter of my life. There is nothing very productive about sitting in your reclining chair and reading or watching television.

For a number of years my children, as well as my other friends and church members have urged me to write a book. A compilation of my sermons was suggested as a possibility. Others thought my life itself was sufficiently interesting to warrant an autobiography. With my daughter, Terri, getting ready to return to Phoenix, the subject came up again. "Why don't you want to write an autobiography"? She asked. My response surprised even me. "Because I am intimidated by what I would have to reveal" I said. When she seemed confused by my answer, I explained.

"In order for an autobiography to have any meaning, other than self-gratification, it must be brutally honest. That is fraught with peril. All your pimples will be on full display. Your failures and foibles must take equal footing with your accomplishments and virtues." Terri paused for a moment and then responded. "Dad, don't you realize that those who love you will not be dismayed to learn that you are human: and if you have critics out there, they are going to think what they want no matter what you say. I think the only thing you need to ask yourself is why you want to write an autobiography; and then say what you want to say." After hugs and tears, she headed back to Phoenix.

After praying about it some more, I decided to try. If it doesn't come together there is no harm done. If it does come together, it may help countless others in their search to find a meaningful relationship with God. It is for that reason I have chosen to call my autobiography, "One Man's Search for God; A Retrospective on Divine Providence."

As I look back over my life, it has become increasingly apparent to me that in each chapter of my life there was an underlying element of Divine Providence that was helping to shape events. Sometimes that is not at all apparent, especially to the casual observer. It only really begins to show itself when you are able to look at a much larger picture; and then, perhaps, only to one who believes in Divine Providence as evidence of God's activity in the world.

I claim no special privilege for God's favor. It is my firm conviction that all who call upon God in sincere and heartfelt adoration will be treated equally as one of His divine creations. Those whose belief systems have not allowed them to do this have only cheated themselves and deprived themselves of the most rewarding of all of life's experiences. I pity them.

It would be impossible to tell my story without starting at the very beginning and leading you through each chapter of my life. In doing this, I will endeavor to be as candid and honest as I can without doing damage to any innocents along the way. Such candor will inevitably result in some embarrassing moments; but when we are wrong, as we all occasionally are, we should be embarrassed. When we are wrong, knowingly or unwittingly, I believe we are judged by what we do to remedy our mistake. Life has a way of throwing us many curve balls, to use a baseball metaphor, and we may not always hit the ball cleanly. When that happens, we have a moral imperative to set it right. To do less would offend the One we are relying upon for preserving our eternal soul.

It is this moral imperative that sets Christians and all other theists apart from agnostics and atheists. There seems to be a growing number who question the existence of God. They are caught on the horns of the dilemma created by the differences between the science and faith communities. The faith community holds tenaciously to the Biblical narrative of creation, the science community believes man evolved from the "soup" of original creation. It's important to note that they don't explain from whence came their "soup". How does SOMETHING evolve from NOTHING? Try wrapping your mind around that concept. That is especially difficult when we behold every day a universe that is so complex. It is composed of thousands of galaxies and a sense of order that boggles our imagination; from the intricacies of millions of insects and other lower life forms to the majesty of man. We marvel at the ability of birds to find their way thousands of miles to the south and then return again to the same nest they used last year. We wonder at dolphins who use sonar for guidance or the miracle of hibernation used by many species. One would think that biologists, as well as other scientists, would be forced to conclude that the existence of God becomes a logical necessity. Of course they might ask "If in the beginning there was nothing except God, then where did God come from?" The truth is that even though the greatest minds in history have pondered that question, no one has found the answer. I believe that no one will. Faith nurtured by the Holy Spirit becomes our window to divine reality.

Even if we see the existence of God as a logical necessity, our acceptance of that reality becomes a matter of faith. As the Apostle Paul said; "Faith is the substance of things hoped for; the evidence of things unseen." (Hebrews 11:1) It is only as that faith takes root in our heart and we truly believe in those things "unseen" that we develop the ability to establish a meaningful relationship with that unseen God. It is a relationship that grows stronger with time and continually renews our confidence that this is the true reality. It is because of this faith that there is a moral and loving God who knows us intimately and knows our every thought and action that we are compelled to follow the dictates of our faith and the commands of the one we accept as the Son of the Father, the Lord Jesus Christ. If we truly believe, it affects every aspect of our lives; our business dealings; our interaction with our neighbors; our relationships within our family and with our spouses; and, yes, even the way we fill out our tax forms.

Compare that with what happens to the agnostic or the atheist. If there is no God and no judgment, then it's every man for himself. Let's get all we can and pursue a life that is filled with as much pleasure as we can muster. When it's over, it's over. There is no tomorrow. That was the philosophy of the Hedonists in early centuries. Hedonism flourished in Rome and Greece through the middle ages and I believe that is where many are today.

It may be that there are many fine people who are agnostics that have responded positively to the culture and social mores of their community. As a result they may do many good and worthwhile things .They may head up public projects; serve as politicians; do charitable work or many other worthwhile things. However, their world view dictates that almost everything must be self-serving. Behind closed doors they seek to promote themselves. What difference does it make if I cheat a little bit in my business dealings? It's permissible to bend the truth a little bit as long as I get away with it. Even if it's a substantive lie, if it works to my benefit, it's alright. If I cheat on my taxes, who cares? Doesn't everybody do it?

If you doubt what I am saying, I suggest you look at today's news headlines, or any day's headlines. If you don't see it there you are blind.

These are the predicates upon which I wish to build as we take this journey together. Each person's search for God will be different and if you are a believer your search may not parallel my own. My hope is this chronicle of my experience will be helpful to your spiritual journey and I trust you will find it interesting.

I was born on July 1, 1933. That means that my history begins long before most of you were even a glimmer in your mother's eye. As we travel together, we will be sidetracking along the way to give you a glimpse into the life and culture of that generation. If you are a fan of some of the old television shows like "Little House on the Prairie", or the myriad of western series, you already have a picture of that time. You may learn a few additional things from my account.

Whenever it is important, I will be pointing to what I believe is evidence of the theme of this discourse, Divine Providence. You will be able to judge for yourselves. I pray it may help you find a more meaningful relationship with Almighty God for yourself, and through you, for those you love and care about. God's love and comforting power becomes ever more powerful as we are able to pass it on. As the poet has said, "God has no hands but our hands to do his work today; He has no feet but our feet to lead men to His way." God bless each one of you. May God's love live and grow in your heart as we take this journey together.

1

Remembering My Ancestors

AS I BEGIN RECREATING MY SEARCH FOR GOD AND A meaningful relationship with the Father who created us, it is essential to remember my earthly ancestors. I was fortunate to have a reasonably good reservoir of information to be able to validate and verify most of what I needed to know about my ancestry. I feel very sorry for the growing number of people who grow up without much knowledge about their history. Broken homes and births out of wedlock are at all-time highs, leaving many only to wonder about their ancestry. So while some of what I am about to tell you may be of little interest to the readers outside my family and circle of friends, it is important. It is important academically and intellectually to know our roots. If I were a racehorse, the first thing the potential owner would want to know is my breeding. He would be very impressed if my sire was Secretariat or any of the Triple Crown winners; other equine fathers might be less impressive. Yet the reality is that many of those others may prove to be better racehorses then those sired by the Triple Crown winners. History has proven that to be true.

Let me say up front that I do not claim any special favor for being related to royalty or publicly famous people. You are hearing from a very common man who comes from a very common heritage. I guess I can claim a very distant birthright for being related on my father's side to John Alden and Rebecca, who came to America on the *Mayflower* and helped found Plymouth Colony. However, that was four centuries ago, and while it may give our children the right to claim membership in the organizations founded as a part of the Mayflower Society, it has limited meaning for today. I make this point because I am confident, beyond doubt, that God has little concern for where we came from or what our earthly circumstances might be. Whoever you are reading this right now, you are as eligible to receive God's favor and blessing as the pope or any of the pastors or ministers that attempt to seek Him out daily. You and I are on a common path. .

My father was born Lloyd Edward Southard in 1896 in Enid, Oklahoma. He was the son of Attison Southard and Etta Shaw. While we do not know all the circumstances or exact dates, we do know that Lloyd's mother and Mr. Southard were divorced and she later remarried a man named John Sample. Lloyd was raised by Mr. Sample, and after being officially adopted, he chose to use his stepfather's name.

We did a genealogy search on Attison Southard and were able to uncover some interesting facts. He served in the military and fought in the Spanish-American War in Cuba. There was a rumor that he married the widow of a wealthy plantation owner in Cuba; but, that is unconfirmed. We do know that he spent the last few years of his life in a veterans' retirement home in Springfield, Illinois. He is buried in their cemetery. A few years ago, my brother, Buddy, made a trip there to see the gravesite and take pictures for our family's historical record. Our research also confirmed that Mr. Southard was our connection to John Alden.

We don't know when, or exactly why, but Mr. Sample ended up in Hutchison, Kansas. Lloyd sent most of his growing-up years there, along with his sister, Mercedes. I recall meeting her one time. When I was about three years old, she visited us in Sidney, Nebraska. All I really remember is that she came bearing gifts. Mine was a truck, and I thought it was the nicest gift I had ever had. I remember Father talking about the fact that she was able to have piano lessons. In those days, only girls were considered eligible to play the piano. Boys needed to be concerned with manly things. My father always resented that because he liked the piano. He said he used to listen to what she learned in her lesson and then, when he was alone, he tried to duplicate it. I do know this. He wowed us every time he sat down at a piano. What little piano I play I learned from him, yet he never had a lesson.

At this point, the family history becomes more complicated and convoluted. I need to begin with my mother's history and then bring the two together. Mother was born Opal Glee Muhr in 1900, the daughter of John William Muhr of Redington, Nebraska. She was the second-eldest daughter of nine children, five boys and four girls. Perhaps my bias is showing, but I would insist that she was the prettiest of the Muhr daughters. Born at the turn of the century, she would not quite live to see a new century, which was her hope. But in her ninety-four years, she made an indelible mark on my life and all those she touched. She was one of those very special people whose commitment to her religious faith and her compassion and empathy for others caused her to be loved by everyone who knew her.

During my childhood years, we had almost no relationship with anyone on Dad's side of the family, but on Mother's side, it was almost continual. Perhaps that was because they were closer to us, or because on Dad's side there was only Mercedes and her children, and they lived way down in Texas. Family reunions on Mother's side were always attended by dozens of people. I think John Muhr must have been related to almost everyone in Morrill County, or so it seemed to me. Most of these reunions were held at a place called Bonners Grove. It was a picnic and camping area not far from Redington. They had a baseball park and other amenities.

Just about everybody in the family enjoyed and played baseball. I was too young to participate, but, I enjoyed watching all of them play. In one game, Uncle Cecil stood at the plate for what seemed an eternity hitting foul balls that all went to the right. Finally, he connected on one and hit a double. Strange the little things that stick in our memories.

One thing I definitely remember is the food. No king's table could be more sumptuous. It may well be that my remembrance of those picnics is colored by the passing of time, but, if I exaggerate, it is not by much. There were always a half-dozen kinds of pie. This has always been one of my weaknesses. My aunt Beryl made a coconut cream pie to delight the taste buds. I remember on one of our trips to her house in Alliance, Nebraska, I ate three pieces. Knowing me and my brothers' love of her pie, she had made four pies. She offered me another slice, but my conscience would not allow it. Later, I wished I had said yes. The large Muhr family brought all kinds of meat dishes and casseroles, and some of them would barbecue. Every picnic ended with huge slices of watermelon, usually offered up later in the day after recovering from a gluttonous afternoon meal. The watermelon was grown locally. Nebraska watermelon rivals the best in the world. It was always sweet and juicy. It was not like what we have been able to buy in the store in recent years.

John Muhr immigrated to the United States from Germany in the 1870s, entering the country legally via Ellis Island. Once here, he did everything according to the book. He learned the language, studied the immigration materials and proudly became a citizen of the United States. Then, he did the most important thing, he assimilated into the culture. I do not ever remember hearing him speak German. He undoubtedly knew it, but only English was spoken in the home. In every respect, John and his children were red, white, and blue Americans.

I feel compelled to take a minute to comment on the subject of immigration. The immigration debate is one of the hot topics of the day. It is creating a lot of division in our country. I think it is important to look to our history and understand what our founders envisioned. Unfortunately, inept or biased teachers, marginal school districts, and, highly politicized administrators have created a generation of young people who are woefully ignorant of their history. According to a study entitled "A survey on patriotism in America" reported by CBS news in November of 2018, this generation of millennials is the least patriotic, the most secular, and the most anti-American in our history. That study claimed that 47% of that age group were no longer proud to be Americans. They believe we are a racist nation and burning the American flag is acceptable. They are part of a larger group that seem determined to tear down our monuments and rewrite our history. We have allowed this to happen.

My purpose here is not to reignite the immigration debate, but I feel compelled to express my opinion about it. It is my firm belief that if we continue to permit pockets of counterculture to foster within our borders, we will live to regret it. I point, for example, to news reports of agitation within the Muslim communities around Dearborn, Michigan, to institute Sharia law for their own community. There is some dispute over those reports, but if they are true this would be an anathema to all constitutionalists. Our constitution and Bill of Rights are the polar opposites of Sharia. If those coming here are unwilling to learn the language and do not wish to share our values, they do not deserve to be called citizens. Let's look at what one of America's heroes had to say on the subject. This is Teddy Roosevelt speaking in 1907.

> "We should insist that if the immigrant comes here in good faith, becomes an American, and assimilates himself to us, he shall be treated on an exact equality with everyone else, for it is an outrage to discriminate against any such man because of creed, or birthplace, or origin. But this is predicated upon

the person's becoming in every facet an American. There can be no divided allegiance here. Any man who says he is an American, but something else also, isn't an American at all. WE HAVE ROOM FOR BUT ONE FLAG, THE AMERICAN FLAG. WE HAVE ROOM FOR BUT ONE LANGUAGE, AND THAT IS THE ENGLISH LANGUAGE … AND WE HAVE ROOM FOR BUT ONE SOLE LOYALTY AND THAT IS A LOYALTY TO THE AMERICAN PEOPLE."

They march every year in California carrying the flag of Mexico. There are many other examples around the country. The New York Yankees and the Philadelphia Flyers have both had a tradition of playing "God Bless America" at each of their games for the past 60 years. Recently, under pressure from well-organized leftist groups, they both caved and discontinued using "God Bless America". They removed their statues of Kate Smith, who introduced the song originally during the 2nd World War. The leftist groups claimed that Kate Smith was a racist because of the lyrics to her song. If Kate Smith is a racist because of the lyrics to "God Bless America", or other of her songs, then every patriotic American is in the same boat. That includes you. We are all racists. That is precisely the point of these leftist attacks. It is their view that all of America is racist. It is their desire to totally rewrite the history of America and replace it with their own vision and world view. Really! Get rid of "God Bless America"! Corrupt and self-serving politicians and educators who are more interested in indoctrination than education have created this mess, and, I fear, it may get a lot worse before it gets better. If we are to preserve the America millions have died to defend, we must stand firm against extremists and overcome their attacks with truth. They seem to be much better prepared for that battle than traditional America. It is time we recognized the threat and gathered the resources to meet the challenge.

John Muhr was one of the original homesteaders in Morrill County, Nebraska. In the museum in Morrill, Nebraska they have one whole wall dedicated to John Muhr. He is revered in that county and is held up as an icon of early Americana. He definitely was a man of influence in the county and his family looked up to him as a great man. There is no doubt, he had many good points. He was an Evangelical Christian, and every Sunday he would load all of the children in the wagon and take them to the little church only a short distance from the homestead. It was there my mother received her spiritual grounding and she clung to the faith of her childhood till the day she died.

We were able to visit the museum few years ago. We arrived there on a Saturday and found the museum closed. As we were about to leave, a lady knocked on our window and asked who we were. We explained that we had heard there was some of our families memorabilia displayed in the museum and we had hoped to see it. She asked what family we were referring to and we said the John Muhr family. Her eyes lit up and she said "Well we have one whole wall dedicated to John Muhr". She explained that she was only there today to catch up on some bookwork but we were welcome to come in. We had the entire place to ourselves. While we already knew most of the information we saw, there was still quite a bit that we learned. The display included a lot of pictures of family. We were duly impressed and grateful to our host for the day.

After the birth of his youngest daughter, Ruby, John Muhrs wife died and he was left to raise nine children alone. Apparently, he placed an ad in one of the farmer's publications seeking a housekeeper and caregiver for his children. At that time, Mr. Sample had passed away and Etta was a widow seeking a source of income. She read the ad and responded to it. To make a long story short, she became the caregiver for nine children in Nebraska. The story becomes more complicated when Etta and John Muhr decide to get married. Ultimately, my dad's mother becomes my mother's stepmother and my mother's dad becomes my father's stepdad. Confused yet? I need to explain how that came to be true.

My father was still living in Hutchison, Kansas .At some point, he decided to sell the small piece of property he owned outside of town and go to where his mother was in Nebraska. After all, he was now Mr. Muhrs stepson and he had heard all the wonderful things about his mother's new husband. Lloyd sold his land and used the money to purchase an automobile which he drove to Nebraska. Once there, he visited his mother at the ranch. According to Mother, Lloyd was a rather dashing young man. She said he was a snappy dresser and wore a fedora hat which was somewhat of a novelty in that area. Our family has a large portrait picture of dad as a young man in his suit and fedora hat. I would have to say he was quite handsome. He must have made an impression on the girls with his clothes and driving an automobile. The horse and carriage was still the primary mode of transport for the farmers and ranchers in that area. Lloyd wanted to stay close to his mother so he found employment in Bridgeport. However, something else was happening. He met a 17 year old beauty, Opal, the third eldest daughter of John Muhr. From what I have been told, it was sparks on both sides from that very first meeting. That first meeting led to a blooming courtship that was resisted vigorously by my grandfather. According to Mother, grandfather did not like my father from the first moment he met him. Perhaps he viewed him as a bit of a rapscallion and he had little to offer in terms of property or potential. Maybe he thought the relationship was too close; or, could it be that something else was bothering him? Could it be that the presence of Etta's son made grandfather uncomfortable because of what was going on with Etta's inheritance at the time? I will detail that a little later in this chapter.

Opal's two older sisters had married ranchers in the area and now she was the primary care giver for the younger children. That could also have been part of grandfather's concern. Etta had developed some health issues which had put the burden of care on

Opal. Despite the hostile protestations of grandfather, Opal and Lloyd found ways to continue their courtship secretly. In 1920 when dad was 24 and mother was 18 they decided to elope knowing that there would never be a blessing from John Muhr. This is the story I have been told about the events of that elopement. Dad drove to the ranch to pick up Opal. I believe they thought they were doing it at a time when grandfather was absent. However, that was not the case. As they were turning the car around to leave the driveway, grandfather came running out of the house with his double barrel shotgun. He fired both barrels directly at Lloyd. His automobile was a convertible and the roof was up. The shot ripped off the roof, but Lloyd and Opal were unhurt. Before grandfather could reload, they were able to exit the yard and drive into Bridgeport where they were married. Thus began a reign of resentment and animus that continued till the day grandfather died.

The unwelcome marriage was not the only reason for bad blood between dad and my grandfather. There was also the question of an inheritance that my father always believed he was entitled to receive. When dad's mother went to Nebraska to work for Mr. Muhr, she had sold the home in Hutchison and some property outside of town and apparently had some other money from the estate. When she arrived in Nebraska, Mr. Muhr, in addition to his work on the ranch, was deeply involved with the Farmer's Union Co-op. We believe he was also an officer of that organization. Apparently, the Farmer's Union Co-op was in financial trouble and badly in need of additional capitol. John Muhr talked Etta into investing all of her money in the Farmer's Union. We don't know what she was promised in return. What we do know is that the Farmer's Union Co-op in Morrill County went bankrupt and she lost all her money. It was a dark shadow that was revisited whenever we would go to a family reunions. I was too young to understand the animus that was obvious between my dad and grandfather. It was never something that mother and dad had discussed with us. All I could do was wonder why Dad would drop us all at the ranch and then drive away not to return until time to go home. I only learned the details of these events when I became an adult.

It was not long after that when Etta passed away without telling Lloyd anything about the transactions with the Farmer's Union. He only learned about it later when he inquired about his anticipated inheritance. He always believed that grandfather had worked his mother to death and had been less then considerate about her health. Grandfather never owned up to any sense of responsibility for what happened with the Farmers Union despite the fact that he helped two of his sons purchase ranches in the area and gave the home ranch to his son Cecil. Opal and Lloyd remained persona non-grata. Even in death, which occurred when I was in high school, he exacted his revenge.

Lloyd and Opal remained in and around Bridgeport for the next several years. During that time their first son was still born. Baby Sample is buried in a family cemetery just three miles from the homestead. They were followed by the birth of my two sisters, Alice and Dorothy and my older brothers, John and Robert. Dad did a lot of different things during those years to provide for his family. He worked for local farmers and ranchers when it was available. He found some work in town and for a time he was a muleskinner digging a canal for the federal government. I have a picture of him driving a six tandem twelve mule hitch pulling a Fresno scraper. Mother did what she could to help out by doing laundry and domestic chores for neighbors. The frosty relationship continued between dad and grandfather. Even when they had some emergencies, grandfather did not offer any help. Opal's brothers and sisters, however, were more generous. John, Cecil, Allen and Alvin all lived in the area and they did not share their father's animus. It's my understanding that their help was minimal, but at least it was something. The stories surrounding those years of struggle are too many to revisit here and would serve no useful purpose outside the family. However, one thing was obvious. Those years of struggle forged a bond between mother and dad that would never be broken. In the years that followed, there were many times when others thought Opal was crazy to stick with Lloyd, but, mother would not permit anyone to speak ill of him and she defended him always. Their love for one another was plain for all the children to see and I am certain that knowledge played a part in the decisions I made later in my own life.

I can summarize, remembering my ancestors, by saying that I am primarily English and Irish on my father's side and German and Scandinavian on my mother's side. We are all children of immigrants, but I am proud of the fact that we are, first and foremost, Americans. While too many do not understand it, that is really what America is all about. As many have said, love her or leave her.

It is not clear to me why, and I don't remember my mother saying, but Mother and Dad moved from Bridgeport to Sidney and lived in an apartment in the old post row of Fort Sidney, one of the original cavalry outposts of the early frontier. It is there that I was born on July I, 1933.

2

My Early Years

ACCORDING TO THE STORY TOLD BY MOTHER AND DAD, I spent the first six months of my life wrapped in cheesecloth. I had been born with a somewhat rare congenital skin disorder known as Ichthyosis and my entire body was covered with open sores. They used the cheesecloth so they could keep the skin moist with calamine lotion. It is a condition that has plagued me for my entire life. It would create embarrassment for me in the boys' locker room trying to explain my fish scale skin. It was also the source for a lot of teasing. Children can be especially cruel. I was always able to find some friends that were empathetic and some of those friends have remained my closest friends over all the years of my life.

My very earliest recollections were when I was three and four years old. We were living in a house on the Northwest side of Sidney, Nebraska. It was located on a rather high hill with open country behind and looked down on the city. Below the yard about 30 feet down was an open field prepared for garden or other cultivation. A full acre was included in Dad's lease and he had taken full advantage of it. Every place we ever lived had to have a large garden space. Mother and Dad relied heavily on what they were able to produce on their own. Mother's pride and joy was her abundance of mason jars for canning. The garden always included peas, green beans, carrots, onions, leaf lettuce, squash, cucumbers, tomatoes, sweet corn, beets, cantaloupe and watermelon. I suspect I am leaving a few things out, but those are the ones I remember. In this garden dad had given my sister, Dorothy, the project of raising the cantaloupe and watermelon. She was going to use it to earn some money, and, I believe it was also part of a project she and her teacher had worked out for her home economics class.

Dorothy worked diligently watering and pampering her garden and the result was astonishing. Even Dad had to admit that the melons looked like the best he had ever seen and a few that had ripened early had already proven that to be true. We had a dog we called Jip. He was ninety- seven varieties of terrier. In other words, he was a mutt, but he had a big bark and he seemed to be always vigilant. One night he set up a terrible ruckus. Dorothy heard him first and ran out of house to see what he was happening. What she saw chilled her bones. A group of ruffian boys from town were in her melon patch busting up her melons with hammers. They had stolen what they wanted to eat, but not content with that they were destroying the rest of them. In her night clothes and slippers, she ran down the hill yelling for them to leave her melons alone. When she reached the field, one of the boys threw his hammer at her hitting her in the face. The blow busted out her two front teeth. She had to wear a partial plate for the rest of her life. By this time Dad had been awakened. He went down to the garden with his gun. By this time the boys had melted into the darkness of the night. Dad was good friends with Sherriff Shultz, but, he was never able to identify the culprits. They had suspicions but that is never enough. Nevertheless, nearly all of Dorothy's beautiful melon garden was destroyed along with her school project. Over the years, this was something Dorothy spoke of frequently. It was, for her, a very traumatic and bitter memory. It was also one of my very earliest memories. All the barking, yelling, and commotion had awakened me. Even though I only looked out the window, I was aware that something bad was happening.

Dad had built shelves in our dirt basement to store whatever they canned, and that was just about everything they produced. Even the corn that was not eaten up fresh was canned or dried. I much preferred the canned. The dried corn just didn't have the flavor. The tomatoes always took several dozen jars. The cucumbers and beets were pickled. I never liked the beets, but most of the family did. Canning time was a big project and everyone in the family participated. In addition to what we grew, dad, who was friends with the store managers of both of the local grocers, Safeway and A. G., would buy cartons of fruit that were too ripe to sell but were still good for canning. He maintained a relationship with both stores by agreeing to come in on snow days and scoop the front of the store. In return, they would sell him the fruit at a good discount or in some cases for free. So the canning time usually included peaches, apricots, apples, sometimes pears, and, always, plums.

Later that summer, when the canning was done and stored away in the cellar, a tragedy occurred. I say a tragedy because that is what is seemed like to me. Dad had discovered that we had at least one rat in the house. He was chewing on some of the potatoes in the cellar. Dad was already a practiced exterminator. Later on he would become exterminator for the city of Sidney. So, dad put rat poison in some strategic places in the cellar and shut the cellar door. No one ever acknowledged their responsibility, but someone left the cellar door open and Jip got into the cellar. The poison is made to be appealing to rats, but apparently it was also appealing to Jip. We found him dead the next morning. He was everybody's dog, but a three year old thinks that he is exclusively his. I was heartbroken.

It is surprising to me how many memories I have of that place at such a young age. We had a neighbor just to the east of us by the name of Bailey. We enjoyed going over to her house because she always had a treat for us. Her son played trumpet in the high school band. After he graduated he went on to form his own dance band. Many years later when I was Pastor in Grand Island, I went to Hastings to hear him play and renew old acquaintances. He remembered me and we had an enjoyable evening.

One of the reasons that memory stands out is because it involved my first recollection of what I would later call sin and redemption. I, and one or two of my brothers, had gone over to the Bailey's to play with the younger children. While there, I had to visit the bathroom. I had been taught always to wash my hands after using the bathroom. This time in the soap dish was a very shiny and pretty ring. I picked it up and put it in my pocket. I later learned it was Mrs. Bailey's wedding ring. When I got home, I couldn't quit thinking about it. I knew it wasn't mine, but what can I do now. Finally, a very remorseful three year old went to Mother and confessed. She was very patient and understanding. She said, march yourself over to Mrs. Bailey and tell her what you did, and tell her you are sorry. I did as I was told and to my surprise Mrs. Bailey was also very kind. In fact, I remember getting a treat. What I remember most is the weight of the world being lifted off my chest. It was my first experience of the spiritual mystery that I would know, as an adult, to be redemption.

Another memory is of my father's illegal poker nights. Gambling was illegal, even social gambling. Of course, I was unaware of it at the time. I only learned the details after I was an adult. Once a week dad hosted a poker night. It included several of the locals and I was told later that some of them were city officials. They needed a place to play where they could be safe from detection and dad needed the income. He would take 10% of every pot. Mother provided sandwiches and drinks. I believe they were soft drinks, but I can't be certain of that. We were never allowed into the living room on poker nights, but sometimes we were able to peek through the keyhole just to see what was going on. I also learned, when I grew up, that dad had for a time, in the early nineteen thirties, run bootleg liquor from North Platte to buyers in Cheyenne County. Sidney's most prominent citizens were the customers. They were probably the only ones that could afford it. During that time, employment was hard to find. We were in the depth of the depression and dad would move heaven and earth to care for his family. Knowing that dad was good friends with the Sherriff, I have always believed that despite its illegality, the prevailing attitude toward social gambling was to ignore it. It was no big deal unless it created a problem and is best left alone. I think that was also true of bootleg liquor. The Volstead Act was repealed in 1933, the same year I was born .Research reveals that after 1930 the public attitude had begun to change. People were convinced the new congress was going to change the law; as a result, prosecution for bootlegging was far less stringent.

Dad's first decent job came when he was hired to sell for Utah Woolen Mills. He came home and proudly displayed his woolen goods to all of us. They had beautiful shirts and scarfs, and women's clothes, and even blankets. He was obviously thrilled. It seemed that everything went well for a while; but, it didn't last. Dad was working primarily, if not altogether, on commission. He had a prospect list which included all the local merchants and a few other regular customers. His first few months he was able to cherry pick. When those leads were gone, and he had to go door to door, the sales grew fewer and fewer until it was no longer sufficient to take care of the family. He had to quit.

After leaving Utah Woolen Mills, Dad was hired to be the exterminator for the city of Sidney. Apparently, the city had developed quite a problem with rats. . Dad had a number of favorite rat stories he enjoyed telling us. His favorite involved the Commercial Hotel in downtown Sidney. It had developed a serious problem with rat infestation. Their basement was alive with them. Dad set about the business of getting rid of them. Using poison and traps he was able to clear most of them out; but, there were a few who seemed to be too smart for the traps or even the poison. When everything seemed to fail, he went to emergency plan B. He consulted with the hotel's management and found a weekend when most of the guests would be gone and the hotel relatively empty. Dad took his pistol and went to the hotel and sat in the basement in the dark with only his flashlight. When he heard a noise that he thought to be a rat, he would shine his flashlight and pick up their gleaming eyes in its light. Dad was an excellent shot. By the end of the night he had bagged more than half dozen rats, and to hear Dad tell it, they were as big as cats. They were certainly the leaders of the pack. The Commercial Hotel had no more rat problem.

When I was four years old my mother enrolled me in kindergarten. I was excited to be starting school because mother had been teaching me my letters and simple math for some time. Dad was a part of that home learning as well. He would play a game where you take two sets of numbers and see who can add them together in their head. I would participate along with my older brothers. As a result, I think I was ahead of most of the children in the class. The schoolhouse was large and foreboding and the children seemed unfriendly. It is strange the things a child would focus on; but, it is those things I remember. For example, I was embarrassed because the other children were coloring in their coloring books with a different kind of crayon than I was using. Mine was a less expensive wax crayon and I could not make my pictures look pretty like theirs. The little girl sitting next to me picked up on my anxiety and began slipping me her crayons to use. It turned out her mother and mine were good friends. She lived right on the street I took to walk home. We became good friends. With mother's permission, I would stop at her house on the way home and play. Her mother usually had a treat for us.

I would only attend that school for two or three months before we moved to the country; but, there is one other memory I need to recall. One day we had a severe thunderstorm. It passed quickly, as most Nebraska thunderstorms do, but it left the roads home from school with large puddles. A four year old cannot resist the temptation to stomp in a puddle. I think I must have stomped in every puddle the entire mile home. When I got home, I was wet and muddy clear to my waist. Mother saw me coming and met me at the door. Needless to say, she was not pleased. Before coming in the house I had to strip off my clothes followed by a quick sponge bath. That was followed by a firm lecture about shoes being expensive as well as good clothes for school. It was a lesson I never forgot.

It came as a total surprise to me when I came home from school one day and was told we are moving to the country. Not someday but right away today. They had been moving our furniture all day. Apparently, the owner of our houhad found a buyer who wanted immediate possession. Dad had done a lot to improve the place as well as the garden plot below the house. It was more desirable than before and we only rented. Dad needed to find a place on short notice. He had a good friend that he played pool with, and I suspect drank with, who was the largest wheat farmer in Cheyenne County. Leon Laffler had several trucks that all carried the Logo "Laffler Farms Cheyenne County". When Dad began looking for a place, Leon said he owned a place seven miles south of town that was empty. He said, "It's not much and the house is not in good repair, but it might suit your purpose". He explained that all the land that was a part of the place was wheat land that he farmed. He had a machine shed on the property where he stored his farm equipment, but he was willing to lease the house and the other out buildings along with a full five acres for garden. Dad jumped at the chance. He was a farmer at heart and his dream had always been to be able to return to the farm. So, in the fall of 1937, we moved to the farm.

That first trip to the farm proved to be an adventure .We were all in the final load along with the three goats. Dad had purchased a goat because my younger brother, Buddy, was allergic to cow's milk. The goat had freshened giving birth to twin kids. They were now six months old and you have never seen a friskier pair. We put them in the back of the trailer along with their mother; but, as soon as we put them in they would bounce right out. Even the high side boards were not enough to hold them .Finally, we tied clothesline rope around their necks and tied them to the side of the trailer. Then, my older brother John sat in the back with all three goats to gentle them. We must have been a sight. I remember the stares as we drove down Main Street and headed south toward County Road 113 with our three goats, the last of the furniture, and a car load of kids.

The farm was located seven miles south of Sidney and one mile from what we called Hand's Corner. The Hand's family owned the largest dairy in the county and supplied most of the milk for Sidney. Just one mile further south was our new home. It was off the road about one quarter mile on a dirt access road that would become a quagmire when it rained. We went bouncing down that lane and got our first view of what would be our home for the next three years. My first impression was that this was wonderful. There was a nice grove of trees right near the house which included, as I later found out, a crabapple tree. The barn looked huge to me and the other out buildings included a chicken house, a hog shed, a machine shed, an outhouse, and a windmill that was quite close to the house. That first impression dampened somewhat when I saw the inside of the house. It was a two story with a single staircase leading to the second floor with its three bedrooms. The walls were totally bare and contained cracks where you could see light coming in from the outside. The only heat was from a stand-up wood and coal stove that we brought with us and the kitchen range which we brought with us as well.

As I look back on it today, I am amazed at how creative and industrious mother and dad truly were. One of dad's friends from town came out and the two of them put mirasko on all the walls. They found ways to cover obvious cracks, repair a leaky roof, and mother used pictures and curtains to turn an old dilapidated farm house into a livable home. We still had some issues with the cracks as we soon discovered. Winter was already upon us and In Nebraska the winter storms can be quite severe. Each time it snowed when there was wind, the snow would drift through those cracks and make little piles of snow on the floor. Three of us boys slept together in one bed. Each night Mother would heat the irons she used in ironing our clothes, wrap them in tea towels and place them at the foot of our bed .When we would leave the warmth of the living room and head upstairs, it would be to a nice warm bed. This very quickly became home.

Dad was still working for the city and had to drive to town each day; but, almost immediately he began to accumulate things that made this seem like a farm. First it was Checko. Checko was a mixed breed of collie with orange, black and white streaks that were very pretty. I have no idea where he came from, but he was a delight. He would be with us for the next ten years. Mother ordered mail order chicks and we built a little area in the house where we could keep them until they were big enough to put in the chicken house.

My oldest sister, Alice, was still in high school and in order to make it easier for her to get to school, she was living in town with her good friend, Virginia Reiker. It is interesting to point out as a side note, that when Alice did graduate from school, she was the Salutatorian and Virginia was the Valedictorian. They studied well together and were inseparable friends. However, Alice, in addition to going to school, was working part time for a local attorney typing his briefs. With the money she earned, she and Dad went to the sale barn and bought a sow that was pregnant. Believe it or not, that sow had 21 little pigs. When those pigs were old enough to sell, they became the source for our first milk cow, Old Red. Old Red, as we called her, was a Jersey- Guernsey mix. She was pregnant when we bought her and when she freshened it was twin heifer calves. Amazingly, over the next several years she gave us four sets of twin heifer calves. We were well on our way to becoming a dairy; but, I can't get ahead of the story.

We had just moved in and we needed to be enrolled in school. John, Robert, and I were still in grade school. My two younger brothers, Buddy and Loren, were not in school yet. There was a country schoolhouse just a mile from the house. It was shorter if you cut across the fields. They had no kindergarten, so after some minor testing, and with the permission of the county superintendent, they put me in first grade. As a result, I graduated first grade one month before my fifth birthday. It's not that I wasn't ready for that. I believe it never bothered me; but, later on in school it always meant that I was the youngest and in most cases the smallest in the class. In high school I went out for football as a senior and I was still only 123 pounds. A defensive tackle of that size is destined to get run over which was quite often my fate when I wasn't sitting on the bench.

School was for me a pure delight, and now in this small school environment, everyone knew everyone, and for the most part we were friends. There was occasional teasing and minor disputes but they didn't last. All together there were only 16 of us in the school. In first grade there were only two; Pete and myself. Pete's dad worked for Hand's Dairy. Pete was somewhat mentally challenged or it's possible that he was mildly autistic. In those days there were no special schools or resources for such children, so here he was in a little country schoolhouse. Nothing came easy for him. He latched on to me like a drowning man. I think I was his only friend. It became a challenge to help him with his lessons. I would walk over to Hand's Dairy and play with Petey and then try to help him with his lesson. The fact that Pete's mother usually had some chocolate milk, a staple at Hand's Dairy, may have been part of that motivation. When I reflected on this time years later, I believe the time I spent mentoring Petey gave me an empathy for others who faced similar issues, including my own sister, Dorothy.

Dorothy was very bright; but, she suffered from grand mal epileptic seizures. This limited everything she did. She would get a job and then have a seizure at work and be out of a job. This happened countless times. It almost got her removed from high school when she had a seizure that scared the kids and the principal wanted her removed. Somehow dad was able to prevail with the superintendent to keep that from happening. Fortunately, as an adult, they had developed medications like Digitalis that could control seizures and Dorothy was seizure free for most of her adult life. Those early days were extremely difficult for her. I don't know how old I was, but, I had to have been quite young, when I became the one to look after Dorothy when she had a seizure. The main thing we had to watch for was to see she didn't swallow her tongue and try to keep her from biting her tongue. It is quite common for epileptic patients to severely harm themselves by biting their tongue. There were many episodes I could relate; but, I think they would serve no useful purpose. Let me simply say that this experience helped set the stage for what was to come years later.

When that first summer arrived, Lloyd set about preparing our garden. He had one of Leon Laffler's men plow the five acres. Everything else was done by hand. We all pitched in to rake it and prepare it for planting. The half-acre closest to the house became the garden. Using hoses leading from the windmill, he set up a simple irrigation system for watering the garden. The rest was planted in potatoes, every bit done by hand. As I recall, it was a beautiful garden and vegetables were plentiful. Meat was a different issue. It seemed that meat was always scarce. Most of it was wild meat. Dad would go hunting for an hour nearly every night after work. Pheasants and bunnies were the main game. Pork and beef were expensive and rarely on the menu. Later on we would have our own pork and beef and would butcher our own and put it in cold storage. As we developed our chicken flock we were able to have a ready supply of chickens and eggs; but, most of that was still a few years away.

John was old enough to be permitted to take the four-ten hunting. Dad had taught him to shoot, as he did all of us as we became old enough. On weekends, when we were not in school, Robert and I, would follow John for miles tramping through the fields and usually we came home with game. The standard rule was, what you shoot, you clean. John did a lot of cleaning. Frequently, we would shoot jackrabbits. Those we did not eat, but Dad encouraged us to get them as tankage for the hogs. They made short work of jackrabbits. I usually got stuck with the chore of dragging the jackrabbit home.

In Dad's rule book, you started out learning to shoot a rifle when you were eight or nine. When you were able to hit a can or bottle in the air with a rifle you could graduate to the four-ten. When you were able to hit pheasants on the fly with the four-ten you could step up to either a twelve or sixteen gauge which would give you greater range. Dad had all those weapons on hand and he taught us all the rules of safety in using them. He was a stickler on enforcing them. One memory regarding gun safety sticks out with me. Starting in the fall of 1938, Dad began hosting all of his friends from town to a hunting party on the first day of pheasant season. Of course, the season had already been open for us all year, but the game warden never bothered us. He only lived a few miles away and I'm sure he had seen us hunting, but he knew we relied on it for food and he left us alone. That first year about ten of Dad's friends showed up including Shag Darnell. Shag was a sergeant on the Sidney police force. Everyone had been hunting all day and I have a picture of everyone lined up with their game. After the pheasants were cleaned mother fried several of them and served everyone a sumptuous meal with potatoes and gravy, pheasant and lots of veggies. That was topped off with her homemade pie.

After dinner Shag decided he wanted to go do some road hunting. He still did not have his limit. For some reason which I cannot remember, I was asked to go along. I was sitting in the front seat watching for game on the right and Shag was watching on the left. We were barely out of the driveway when Shag spotted a rooster crossing the road. One of Dad's rules was, if you are road hunting, you do not load the gun till you are out of the car. Shag had his double barrel shotgun open, but it was loaded. He slammed on his brakes, grabbed his gun and in the same motion closed it. Both barrels discharged into the floorboard of the car. No one was hurt, but it frightened me. Shag decided he had enough hunting for the day and we returned to the house. When Dad learned what happened, he was furious. I heard him tell Shag," You are a police officer. Don't you follow the simple rules of gun safety? My son could have been seriously hurt." I believe Shag and dad remained friends after that because Shag came again the following year; but, it reinforced for me the importance of gun safety.

Saturday's were always bath day and washing day. Alice was in charge of the baths. A large tub of water was placed in front of the kitchen range with the oven door open for heat. One by one we would bathe and wash our hair. Loren and Buddy were small and would bathe together. After the boys, the girls would bathe and mother would be last. I think they changed the water for the older ones, but I know the boys all bathed in the same water. I always wondered when Dad bathed. I'm sure he must have, but I was never aware of it. Perhaps he did it after we were in bed. After the baths came laundry time. We had a push-pull washer that we took turns using. Each load took fifteen minutes; then the clothes had to be rinsed, squeeze dried, and hung on the clothesline. The washer was hard to push and pull so this was never a chore I relished. It was mainly the older ones that did it; but, I did it enough to know I didn't like it.

Alice had been a stalwart partner in making everything work. In addition to all she did to help mother, she had helped out financially as well; but that was about to change. She came home one day with news that she had been offered a wonderful job working for the superintendent of schools in Curtis, Nebraska. She felt she had to accept. I always believed that part of her motivation was to get away from Bernie. Bernie was a local boy that had been sweet on Alice for a long time. He was so persistent that Dad regarded him as a pest. He would come charging up the road in his Model A. As he would come near the yard, he would hit the spark so the car would backfire. The loud noise would scatter the chickens and the dog would bark. Bernie thought it funny, but Alice was never amused. Several proposals of marriage had already been turned down. Going to Curtis put distance between them. Alice was out of our lives for a while.

That was to be short lived. It seemed no time at all when we got the telegram that informed us that Alice had been married. She had met John Adams, the son of a retired local teacher. They had fallen in love and had just been married. Johnny had his B.A. degree from the University of Nebraska and was planning to go on to graduate school. The telegram said they were going to be coming through Sidney on the Union Pacific on their way to California for their honeymoon. Alice wanted Mother and Dad to meet Johnny. Despite their great disappointment that Alice had not included them in her wedding, they made plans to meet the train. I'm certain that Alice did it the way she did because she believed it would work a hardship on Mother and Dad to go to Curtis. After they met Johnny, Dad and Mother were quite relieved. They thought he seemed to be an excellent choice for Alice. They left for California with Dad's blessing.

A few months after their return from their honeymoon, we received news that was quite concerning. Europe was already erupting in armed conflict with Hitler's armies invading and taking control of neighboring countries. The threat of potential American involvement was very real and Johnny was in the National Guard. His unit had been called up and he was to report for active duty forthwith. Alice came home to live with us, and, she informed the family that she was pregnant. She would remain with us through the birth of her first son, John Jr., and then till John's return after his term of service. There is much more I could tell you about those years with Alice and Little John; but, I fear I am becoming too verbose.

So far, I have been focusing primarily on Dad and other members of the family with very little about Mother. Yet she was the cement that held it all together. When we moved to the farm Mother was still a young woman, only 37 years old. She had been married to Dad since she was eighteen. In that time she had birthed seven children and one still born for a total of eight. She had raised and nurtured them and still had time to do many of the manly chores that needed to be done. She was not only a beautiful woman, she was strong and resilient. She was only four feet eleven inches tall; but, she was all heart as this next story will tell you. One day I was playing in the yard. John and Robert were gone, probably hunting. It was ironing day and mother had her kitchen stove stoked up to heat her irons. I looked up and saw that sparks from the chimney had set the roof on fire. Breathlessly, I ran in the house and told Mother. She ran out and looked and immediately said, "Run to Hand's corner and tell them to call the fire department." I ran all the way. After telling them, I started running back home. Before I could get there, the fire truck went around me. He was followed by the Deputy Sherriff who stopped and picked me up and drove me back to the house. When we got there, Mother had already put the fire out. She had the ladder up against the side of the house, but it didn't quite reach the roof. Yet she had managed, single handed, to carry water, climb up the ladder, somehow get on the roof and dump water on the fire. We learned later that it took multiple trips and several falls off the roof to get the fire out. The fire chief was amazed. I remember that he made one more trip to the roof with a bucket of water just to make sure. The wind was blowing and he got most of the water in his face. I thought that was pretty funny. The next week on the front page of the Sidney Telegraph, the local paper, was the headline story. "Local farm woman saves home from fire." Yes, my mother was one tough lady.

Not only was she tough, she was an excellent cook. One of my fondest memories was coming home from school to the smell of fresh cooked bread or cinnamon rolls. All of our bread was homemade. As long as Mother had flour and her yeast cake, we would have bread .Yeast cake was only 3 cents. I wonder what it is today. To assure that we had flour, Mother and Dad would spend every weekend, during and after wheat harvest, gleaning wheat from Leon Lafflers fields. They took a page right out of the Bible and gleaned many bushels of wheat. The wheat was then taken to Sitz Mill in Sidney for grinding and processing. Some was easy ground. That was going to be used for hot breakfast cereal. It was quite good with cream and a little honey or sugar. The rest was made into flour. Aha! Bread, pancakes, biscuits, and, yes, cake. We were becoming more independent all the time. The depression had been hard on everybody, but I know there were many others much worse off than we were. I always wondered why they were not more resourceful in taking care of their own needs. Any small patch of ground can grow a garden with a little effort. It just always seemed that many people were too quick to rely on someone else to take care of them.

The fall of 1938 turned out to be a hard one for us. We had no sooner had all Dad's friends in for the opening of pheasant season when Dad was informed that the city of Sidney no longer needed an exterminator. Out of work again right before Christmas. All I really remember is the events of Christmas Day. I don't know what Mother had planned for dinner; probably, one of her prized laying hens. They were Mother's pets. Whenever it became necessary for us to kill one of them for a meal, it would break her heart. She had no problem with killing a rooster or a hen that was unproductive, but not her laying hens. My brothers and I were in the machine shed playing that morning when we looked out through a crack in the wall and saw a Canadian goose sitting on a straw bale only a short distance in the field. He just seemed to be sitting there without a care in the world. I ran into the house and told Dad what we had seen. He could hardly believe it. We rarely saw geese in that area. Dad grabbed his rifle and came out to the shed. The goose was still there. Dad took aim for what seemed an eternity, but after one shot we had a goose for Christmas dinner. I remember how good the dressing was made with the heart, liver, and gizzard of the goose, and I remember the blessing mother said over Christmas dinner. She declared Mr. Goose to be a heaven sent gift from the Lord. I, for one, believed her.

My memories from 1939 are somewhat limited. I remember being deathly ill from eating too many crabapples from our crabapple tree, and, suffering severe hay fever from running into the fields of green wheat. I would have to lie on the floor with cold compresses on my eyes until the swelling would go down. I remember Dorothy's incident with the badger. The badger had gotten into the pen where Dorothy was raising some baby turkeys. He had killed some of them and Dorothy was furious. She took the shotgun and we began a badger hunt. She gave Checko the scent and he took off at a dead run. He ran all the way to the end of our driveway and there in the borrow pit he stopped and started digging in a hole. When we got there he had already dug far enough in to rouse an angry badger. As you may or may not know, an angry badger can be extremely dangerous. Not just for dogs, but people as well. Without blinking an eye, an angry Dorothy stuck the barrel of the shotgun into the hole and fired. She got the badger .Later when Dad found out, he said she was lucky the gun didn't blow up in her face. The good news was, next Christmas we would be able to have turkey for dinner.

The main thing I remember about 1939 was finding out we would have to move again. Leon Laffler wanted to buy a huge new tractor that he believed would greatly increase his productivity. Even though Leon had excellent credit, at the end of the depression the banks had no money to loan. If Leon wanted his tractor he would need to sell some property to get the cash. The easiest to sell was our place. Dad had greatly improved the house, built a new chicken house, established an excellent garden, and improved the access road. The place seemed very appealing to the Krinebring family, German immigrants with a large family. Leon was very apologetic to Dad, but he did not renew our lease which was up at the end of October. We had one more pheasant season with Dad's friends. It was always the last Saturday in October in Nebraska. Fortunately, Dad was aware that the Gus Nargess farm was vacant. That was the farm just to the south of us, only three quarters of a mile down the road. Gus Nargess was a German immigrant that we found out later was under suspicion by federal authorities of having ties to the Nazi's. Nothing ever came of that, so I assume the suspicions were unfounded. Mr. Nargess agreed to lease Dad the farm along with a hundred acres of pasture for the cattle in our growing herd. The move was simple and the house was much nicer than where we were It even had a pump in the kitchen. No more running to the well for water. We also liked the fact it had a cistern near the windmill that provided water for the garden and was also big enough for swimming. It did not contain drinking water. That came from a different line; so, it was alright for us to swim in it and we did. We would frequently invite our neighbor friends to join us for a swim. It was always cold water, but we enjoyed it anyway. The girls would sometimes get shocked by what I think were salamanders that would occasionally show up in the water. They were black and bright orange. I can't say I was too fond of them either.

We were able to continue at the same school without interruption only now we were just a quarter of a mile from the Hemmerwrights. Their three children went to school with us. Robert was sweet on Ramona their eldest daughter. Before we always cut across the fields to go to school; but now we could walk on the road with the Hemmerwrights. We were just about one hundred yards south of the mile road that led directly to the school. Our mail box was on that corner and there was a grove of trees next to the road between the mailbox and home. Each day, Robert would walk with Ramona. This home brings back a swarm of old memories. I will recount only a few of the most important, or at least the most important from my perspective. In retrospect, I have to wonder about the way it all came to pass with the expediency of this new move. Was there a divine element to it? Was it Mother's strong faith in the power of God to help provide? Was it just Dad's dogged persistence; or was it just plain good luck? I have my own opinion.

The place had a nice chicken house and also a large barn with an area for milking the cows. By now we had been able to add to the herd with some more milk cows plus the ones we raised along with an Ayrshire bull. This was the year we first began selling milk and eggs in town. We now had a sizable flock of chickens and laying hens. They were producing much more than we could use, so we began selling them in town. The milk that was being produced at night we would use for ourselves and the calves and the pigs. All the milk that was not for human use we would put through a separator to extract the cream. The morning milk we would bottle in gallon, half gallon, or quart mason jars to be sold in town. That meant that all of the cows whose milk was being sold had to be inspected by the state. They had to have Mastitis and Tetanus vaccinations and be clear of any other diseases. To begin with, all of our sales were by word of mouth. Many people wanted whole raw milk and not pasteurized milk. People quickly learned that we had whole milk and cream and eggs for sale. We had more customers than we had product. The Sample Dairy was just beginning. Later we would have fresh butter, buttermilk, and young frying chickens; but that was still a way down the road. The biggest challenge now was providing feed for the chickens, grain and hay for the cattle and food for the hogs. All of those things were expensive by the standard of the day. It meant that Dad had to continue work in town and Mother and the three older boys had to be responsible for feeding the livestock, milking, separating and bottling the milk and then delivering it to town. We all had our assigned duties, but Mother had to be the one doing all the delivering along with all her other responsibilities. I truly do not know how she did it.

Somewhere in this time frame, Dad had begun working for Western Ice. This was a plant for making ice to sell. Dad helped freeze the ice. This was also a cold storage facility where you could rent a locker for storing your frozen goods. Dad got a locker as part of his work, so now we had a place for our butchered meat and for frozen vegetables. They also were a large warehouse facility for the local grocers and other wholesale companies; notably. Budweiser, Schlitz, and other breweries. Dad, along with several others, was responsible for loading and unloading the trucks. It was backbreaking work; but, dad did it without complaining. The pay was good for that time and we desperately needed it.

It was at this house that I became more acutely aware of the war. I enjoyed, when I had time, just sitting under one of the trees north of the house and day dreaming. One day, while sitting there, I was startled out of my overalls by a group of four or five airplanes that came swooping past not more than one hundred feet off the ground. I later learned that they were fighter planes from Lowry Air Base in Denver. They were practicing their strafing and bombing runs. Another sharp reminder came one Sunday morning when a group of several Indians came wandering into the yard. I know it had to be a Sunday because Dad was home and that was the only day of the week when he could be at home. The Indians explained that they were on their way to work at the Sioux Ordinance Depot which was an ammunition storage northwest of Sidney. They were from the Rosebud Indian Reservation and they said they were cat skinners. They wanted water as they were on foot and had been walking for a long distance. Dad went in and spoke with Mother and then came out and asked if they would like to stay for dinner. They gratefully accepted, ate their dinner and then went on their way. After they left I asked Dad a question. "Dad, why are cat skinners needed in a war. What are skinned cats used for?" Dad patiently explained, they don't skin cats. The cats they refer to are caterpillar tractors used for construction and road building. I was very relieved. I had been trying to imagine a world without cats.

Later on, I'm not certain of the dates, the Sioux Ordinance Depot would again become a factor in our family history. The Depot was expanded to become a prisoner of war camp for Italian prisoners of war. Probably the work of those cat skinners we had hosted a year or so earlier. My sister, Dorothy, was hired to be the chief cook for the Italian prisoners. Fortunately, she never had one of her seizures while working there; at least, none that I knew about. Dorothy related one rather humorous story about her experience there. The prisoners would help out in the kitchen and other chores around the camp. For the most part, they were very well behaved and Dorothy got the distinct impression that their heart was not really in the war. They seemed to be glad to be out of it alive and they had no love for Hitler or even El Duce. However, they were into complaining about the food. The primary staple being supplied by the government was potatoes and several of the prisoners had been assigned the duty of peeling them. They did not speak much English, but they were able to speak enough to say "potate, potate, potate; never no spaget." Apparently spaghetti was not readily available, or else it just wasn't on the governments menu. She had to use what was sent to her. One day Dorothy took it upon herself to purchase enough spaghetti to make a good meal for all the prisoners. She had the meat and other ingredients available to her. Her meal was a prison wide success and her popularity went up several notches with the prisoners. She worked there till the end of the war.

It was during this time that Dorothy came driving up the road in a Nash automobile. She truly did need transportation for work. The only way she could get there or back was to have Dad take her. She got to within 100 yards of our driveway when the car quit and she had to walk into the yard. Dad was totally flabbergasted. Dorothy was just recently of legal age and she had never driven except around the farm, and she had no driver's license. A salesman at the dealership in town had talked her into putting up a down payment and went ahead and sent her home with the car which they believed made her legally responsible. Dad, as you might expect was furious. He had already been told that Dorothy could not qualify for a driver's license because of her Grand Mal seizures. Somehow, Dad got the car back into town and to the dealership. I would have loved to have been a little mouse listening to the ensuing conversation. I am certain one salesman's ears are still burning. The bottom line is, they took the car back and refunded Dorothy's down payment. It would be quite a few more years before Dorothy was able to drive legally. Her transportation problem had to be solved by taking a room right at the Ordinance Depot. Dad was her transportation otherwise.

Another reminder of the war occurred at our school Christmas program that year. Each year the school would have a Christmas program including all the children. The parents would all be there and each child would receive a gift bag of goodies; usually, fruit, candy, and nuts, handed out by the school supervisors; all farmers in the area. One of the guests that night was Chuck Laffler. He and his younger brother, Raymond, were our friends and we had attended Halloween parties with Chuck. Now he was a fighter pilot flying P52's. When he drove into the school yard that night he must have thought he was flying his plane because the car flew into the yard and everyone was aghast. Chuck looked so dapper in his uniform and pilots hat that no one had the heart to criticize. Twelve years ago, my brothers, Buddy and Loren, and I made a trip back to Sidney to revisit old memories and Chuck again became part of it. First we went to what had been the Krinebring place. There was now a gate at the entrance to the driveway. We climbed over and walked down to the house. It was in total shambles; but the yard was just filled with old cars many of which seemed to be race cars. After taking a lot of pictures we made our way out of the yard and proceeded to the Gus Nargess place. It was totally gone. All the buildings were gone and even the windmill. It was now all one continuous wheat field. We were about to leave when a pickup pulled up and blocked our path. A man got out and came to my window. I was driving. He looked at me and said, "You must be Rex". I looked at him and said, "And you must be Raymond. "It had been sixty years. Wow! Raymond explained that he saw us go into the Krinebring place and then go over to where the Gus Nargess place had been and he had put two and two together and concluded it must be us. He went on to say that we were very lucky because

Chuck lived in the place on the hill just past Hands and he watched the place like a hawk. He was not mentally right in and he had been taking shots at people that entered where we had been. Raymond explained that the Lafflers had been able to repurchase the place from the Krinebrings many years ago and Chuck had lived there during his racing career. He became a race driver after the war racing at dirt tracks around the country. Most of those cars were ones he raced and he guarded them jealously. We thought about going to see Chuck, but Raymond thought it was not advisable, so we didn't. One thing for certain, Laffler Farms still farm Cheyenne County.

One incident stands out in my memory during our tenure at the Nargus place. One day my brothers and I were in the grain bin looking for a watermelon for Sunday dinner. That requires a little explanation. The grain bin was used by Mr. Nargus as one of his wheat storages. We took advantage of that in using the wheat to preserve some food. At the end of the gardening season, we would pick all the remaining watermelon and cantaloupe and cover them with wheat. We were able to keep them good till long into the winter. We did that with unshucked roasting ears as well. They did not keep as long, but it would give us sweet corn for Thanksgiving. On this day we were digging for a melon. We had been using them regularly, so we had to dig a little deeper. It was then we heard the sound of a car coming down the road toward our driveway. I, immediately jumped up and said, Grandma and Grandpa are here. My brothers looked at me like I was crazy and said, no they're not; but, when we got out of the bin, we saw Grandma and Grandpa drive into the yard. Again my brothers looked at me and asked, how did you know? I had to say, I don't know. They had never come to see us before, not even when we had been desperate. That day they were there for only long enough to eat dinner and have some conversation with Mother and Dad while we all played in the yard. I never knew what that was about. I tend to believe it was because two of mother's brothers were about to leave for military duty in the war. I do know that Mother made a trip to Bridgeport shortly after that.

The point of telling you this story is because as minor an incident as this was it sticks in my memory and illustrates a reality that is often ignored or overlooked. I believe most of us, likely you included, have experienced that sudden moment or flash of insight when you suddenly knew something you didn't know you knew. Psychologists have called it precognition. The tendency is to shrug our shoulders and pass it off as just a coincidence. It is generally ignored. The truth is, we utilize only a small portion of what the human mind is capable of doing. The entire field of Gestalt psychology which arose starting in 1890 has demonstrated this to be true. While I have seen no specific studies to refer to, I believe there is a connection between that psychic phenomenon and the power of prayer. Our agnostic or atheistic friends will tell you that prayer is nothing more than your own wishful thinking put into religious language. Christians can point to thousands of examples demonstrating the power of prayer. Many people offering up the same sincere prayer become a mighty bulwark. Then, why you ask, do some prayers seem to be left unanswered. I don't know the answer. Only God knows; but, I can give you some guidelines. The best one is the one that Jesus gave us. Go back and repeat your Lord's Prayer to yourself and really hear what it is saying. No place did I read "Lord give me that new Ferrari". We will talk more about this later. Just let me say for now that prayer, to be effective, must include three basic elements. A valid petition, a genuine and sincere petitioner, which assumes a person of faith who believes in this power, and the divine affirmation of God. If any of those elements are missing, so is the prayer.

In the fall of 1942 our lives changed again. Because of the war, the price of wheat was skyrocketing. All available land was being plowed up for wheat. Gus Nargess decided he needed to plow up our pasture for wheat. He didn't end our lease, but Dad knew that without pasture for the cattle it just wouldn't work. Again a little foresight and anticipation paid off. Dad had almost expected this to happen because our pasture was readily susceptible to tilling. He had been doing some preemptive looking. He knew he needed a place with a lot of pasture, but pasture that would not be plowed up. That was a tall order in that area, but Dad found it. There was a farm that was vacant right near the edge of town that had over 200 acres of pasture that extended into the hills east of Sidney. They would be good pasture and not suitable for tillage. The place also had about 60 acres south and east of the house that would be suitable to grow corn or cane. He was successful in negotiating a lease and we moved lock, stock, and barrel to our new home.

The property was situated just east of town. The street in front of the house was paved. One half mile to the east it hit the highway going north to Bridgeport. Going west it went into town; or, you could go south just ten or 20 yards past our driveway and cross the Union Pacific Railroad and hit the main highway going into town. Either way led you past the local cemetery, which would play a part in some of the stories surrounding our time here. The house was the nicest I had ever lived in. The best part was electricity and indoor plumbing. We had not had those in years. Plus, it was connected for phone. It was for us like moving into the Taj Mahal. The barn was ideally set up for our dairy operation and there was plenty of room for the hogs and chickens. As I look back now, I can only conclude that some power beyond our own was looking out for us. This place was perfect and why did it become available at just the right time?

It became immediately apparent to Dad that he was going to need some additional things quickly. He was able to convince Albin Olsen, local supervisor for the Federal Land Bank, to loan him enough money to purchase two teams of draft horses, some basic pieces of machinery, including a plow, a rake and a planter. He also purchased a hayrack and an International pickup; and, yes, a few additional milk cows. Albin Olsen, was the largest alfalfa farmer in the area. His was an irrigated farm just west of town, and Dad had been purchasing what alfalfa we were able to afford from him. It was a little past normal planting time, but Dad was determined to try to get a late crop of cane going so we could have winter feed for the cattle without having to purchase it. With mothers help and some help from John, he was able to plow and plant cane in the plot of ground that was east of us across the highway. When the cane matured, I don't remember who or how it got cut, but I know we gathered all the bales by hand and hauled them to the barn on the hayrack. There was snow on the ground before we got done, but the cattle had winter feed.

I was still in grade school, of course, as were my little brothers, Loren and Buddy. We were enrolled in Sidney Grade School. Robert was in Middle School and John in High School. My memories of that school are very repressed and unclear. Attending there had been like culture shock. Before, it had been just me and Petey. Now I felt like a duck out of water. All the kids were strangers. Fortunately, the three of us had each other, and this became a time of bonding with Loren and Buddy that brought us much closer together. Our entire family has always been very close; but, I think these years generated a special bond between Loren and Buddy and myself.

Our day would begin at 4:30 a.m. If we were the one designated to bring the cattle in for milking. If it was not our day, we could stay in bed another half hour till five. Then it was milking time. All of our cows were milked by hand. The big dairies had electric milking machines, but that was never within our reach. We were now milking about 20 head. John, Robert, Dad, and I were the milkers. Now that we lived so close to town, Dad could help with the milking and still get to work. Mother would step in if anyone was missing. It gave us about four apiece. Dad was fast and I was slow. My hands would start to ache. Dad probably ended up doing one or two of mine. Loren and Bud were assigned to feed chickens and hogs and whatever else needed doing. When the chores were done, the milk bottled and ready for delivery, we all sat down together for a country breakfast. Breakfast tastes so much better after a couple of hours of work. So many of the children being born today have no concept of what that is all about. There is a sense of pride and a feeling of accomplishment that comes from being a part of helping to make it work for the family. One for all and all for one. It has continued to be our motto through the years.

As soon as breakfast was over it was a mad dash to get to school, get Dad to work, and, get Mother started with her deliveries. Mornings were always a challenge in our home at that time. Just not enough hours for what needed doing. The evening milking began at five. Dad would sometimes be there in time to help, but, when he was not Mother again filled the breach. As soon as the cows were all milked, Mother would go in to start supper and we would finish up the feeding, separating the cream and whatever else needed doing. We would then sit down and listen to Mothers blessing before enjoying supper together. Evenings were for school work and listening to some old time radio. Our favorites were "One Man's Family", "Major Bowes and the Amateur Hour", "Jack Armstrong, "Sky King" and "Fibber McGee and Molly". Oh, and I can't forget, "I Love A Mystery". Its eerie theme music of "Intersanctum" could send chills up your spine. The imaginary world they were able to create in the mind of a child with old time radio is in many ways unmatched with modern television.

Our second year in this new location brought an event that I would single out as the highlight of my growing up years. It was a total and complete surprise. One Sunday afternoon mother and dad said they had to leave, but they would be back in a little while. They had been acting a little mysterious for a couple of days whispering back and forth and kids are always curious about what's going on. They drove out of the driveway and went to the corner west of the house; but, instead of turning to go into town they turned north and we had no idea why and we began speculating to each other. We had stewed in our own juice for over an hour when mother drove into the yard alone. We all rushed out and said, "Where's dad?" She said he would be there in a little bit. Almost before she got it said, Dad came proudly riding in on what I thought was the most beautiful horse I had ever seen. She was a half Arabian and half Indian Paint. He had purchased her and the saddle and bridle from a neighbor that lived about two miles north of us. We decided to name her Pixie because of the proud and spirited way she held her head, and we learned later that she was five gaited. In addition to walk, trot, pace, and gallop, she was also a single footer. That is a gait that is very comfortable for the rider and is not common; however, it is highly prized by horse people. For me it was love at first sight. I couldn't wait to ride her. Before we could do that, we had to listen to a little lecture from Dad. He explained that he was going to put the saddle in the barn and we were not to use a saddle until he said we could use it. It had been only a short time since our Uncle Cecil, Mother's brother, had been seriously injured because he was unseated from his horse, got his foot caught in the stirrup, and was dragged almost to death before granddad had been able to rescue him. Dad said we should hang onto the mane to keep from falling off; but, if we did fall off, it would be a clean fall.

Over the next several years we all became excellent riders, and Pixie was a marvel. She obviously loved all of us, and she loved the attention she received. To say we spoiled her would be an understatement. We all used Pixie to bring in the cattle. Our largest pasture was east of the highway. You had to go a quarter mile north of the house, take a right and go down a fifteen foot wide causeway, go under the highway through a ten foot tunnel, and then you were in the east pasture. That pasture had the most grass plus a little pond, so that's where the cattle and the horses usually could be found. Pixie was a trained cattle pony, so she knew better what to do with the cattle than we did. After a few months, it was not uncommon to see me riding Pixie to get the cattle with no bridle. She knew exactly what she was supposed to do, and, she would do it. Yes, I did fall off a few times. Pixie could turn on a dime if one of the cattle got out of line, and, if you weren't ready you would end up on the ground. Whenever it happened to me, Pixie would stop and come back to where I was, put her head down to see if I was hurt with that what in the world are you doing look on her face. She would patiently wait for me to get back aboard and then we would be off again. She belonged to all of us; but just like Jip and Checko, in my mind, she was especially mine.

I mentioned earlier that we were just a stone's throw from the local cemetery and over the next two years it was the source of some interesting experiences. Kids have a way of conjuring up all kinds of imaginary images of spooks and goblins and what better place than the cemetery. This one did not have a front gate, so anyone could just drive in or walk in. We were only there a short time before we had to go investigate the cemetery at night. It was great fun playing hide and seek in a really spooky place; but we soon learned that this was a popular destination for the older high school crowd. More than once we were in the cemetery playing when all the headlights would show up and it would be a group of high school kids with their dates. It was also used for hazing or initiation pranks for FFA and other school organizations. Whenever there was something going on in the cemetery, we could hear it from our bedroom just across the street; and what a great place to tell ghost stories!

We lived here enjoying the progress we were making for the next two and one half years when our fortunes changed. The owner decided to put the farm up for sale. I don't know the price he was asking, but I do know that Dad was determined to buy it. It was working perfectly for our purposes and it was close to town. With the money that Dorothy had been able to put in the family pot plus what the dairy had generated, along with his own salary, Dad had seven thousand dollars in the bank for a down payment. He set about trying to find financing to purchase the farm. The local bank and the savings and loan both turned him down. He then turned to the man he considered his good friend, Albin Olsen, and the Federal Land Bank. After they finished their review, Albin told Dad, "Lloyd, I am going to do you a favor. That land isn't good for anything but cockleburs. I believe that it is in your best interest that I turn you down." Dad made all the arguments he was able to muster to convince him otherwise; but, it was all to no avail. Meanwhile, someone else stepped up to the plate and bought the farm. I always suspected that Albin was a part of that or that maybe he himself had purchased it. I don't know. Dad never spoke to him again and we went as far away as Sterling, Colorado to purchase alfalfa rather than buy it from Albin. When we were back in Sidney a few years ago, we found that the land directly south of the house that had been our corn field, now has a million dollar natural gas plant from several gas wells on the property. The east pasture on the other side of the highway has three producing oil wells. I don't think it is unreasonable to smell a rat; but, that is only a suspicion.

When we speak of Divine Providence, we always need to remember that we are never going to understand why some things work out the way they do. You would think that in a perfect world, Divine Providence would have dictated that Mother and Dad, who had worked so hard to get where they were, would get their loan, buy the farm, and as they say in the story books, live happily ever after. It did not happen. Are we therefore to conclude that Divine Providence was not present in this case? It is the age old question that theologians have been asking for generations. Why do bad things happen to good people? I will have more to say about that in a later chapter; but don't skip ahead.

We now needed to find another option. There were few choices. Dad settled on moving to a farm that was located back out south on County Road 113. This one, however, was just four miles out of town. It was less than ideal. The house was fine, but there was only one small pasture of about fifty acres. That meant we would have to supplement their feeding another way. Dad had been able to negotiate grazing rights for the stubble fields that surrounded the place, but the cattle would need to be physically herded to keep them together. There were no fences. They also had to be kept off the green wheat fields. Green wheat would cause bloating and possible death. We would need to bring the cattle into the corral and feed them over night with cane and alfalfa and prairie hay. All the feed would need to be purchased. There was one positive to the night feeding. The morning milk was for selling and the night feeding produced better milk. We all pitched in to help herd the cattle; even Dorothy. During the next two years, Pixie more than earned her keep. She was a magnificent cow pony. All you had to do was stay aboard and she would do the rest. She always seemed to know just what you wanted.

I was now in sixth grade. The second half of my school year would be completed at another small country school house just a mile from the farm. It was like coming home. We fit right in and felt comfortable from the first day. The kids seemed to be grateful for some new blood. Somebody else to play softball with at recess time. It was here I saw my first Coleman Scooter. Ronald Paris rode a scooter to school, and I was envious. I spoke with Mother and Dad and asked if we could ride Pixie to school on days when the cattle were in the pasture. After some brief discussion about her care, they agreed. We must have been a sight. I rode in front with Loren and Buddy behind me. Pixie would be tethered in back of the school where there was good grass for grazing and we set up a barrel for watering. Ronald was envious of Pixie. We exchanged favors. Ronald was permitted to ride Pixie and I got to try out the Coleman Scooter. We became very good friends.

It was during this time frame that another harsh reminder came that America was at war. Brother John had graduated from high school and desperately wanted to join the war effort. He had tried the army, navy, and marines, but had been turned down by them all. This was because of his disability. He only had one eye. When John was only four years old, doctors had removed one eye because of an infection they felt could move to both eyes and leave him blind. Dad always regretted having given permission; but, it would affect all the rest of John's life. John's best friend was

Howard Hershberger. He lived in town but would come out to the farm sometimes on weekends to see John and they would go hunting together. Dad did not care for Howard. He thought he was irresponsible and not a good influence on John. He caught them smoking one day and I suspect this colored Dad's opinion. By today's standards that wouldn't rank very far up there on the no no's list.

One day John turned up missing. All day everyone stewed and fretted about where he had gone. Late that evening he came home. He and Howard had gone to Sterling, Colorado. It had the nearest recruiting office for the Merchant Marines. They had gone to enlist; but, John was crestfallen. Howard had been accepted but he had again been rejected. I am certain that this experience explains some of the things that would occur in John's life later on. Howard was off to war and John was stuck at home. It seemed to me it was no time, but I'm certain it had to have been quite a few months, when word came that Howard had been lost at sea. His merchant vessel had been torpedoed by German submarines and sunk losing all hands. I know this had a profound effect on John.

For some time it seemed everything was going to work out fine. The dairy was doing well and Dad was able to stay at home and work the farm full time. Our bottom line was being affected by the high cost of feed for the cattle; but, we were now offering butter and buttermilk as well as eggs and chickens and even rabbits. I had developed a little rabbit project of my own raising white rabbits. For me they were all pets. We never, ever, had one of them on our dinner table; but, they were a surprisingly popular choice for some of the folks in town, and they bought all we could supply. We would remain here through my sixth, seventh, and eighth grade; however, for eighth grade I had to go into town to middle school.

Then came the bombshell. The State of Nebraska passed the pasteurization bill. No longer would anyone be permitted to sell raw milk such as we were doing. It would still be legal for someone to drive out to the farm and buy raw milk in a one on one transaction, but no more of what we were doing. This meant that we would have to set up a pasteurizing facility which would be extremely expensive or, sell all of our milk to one of the large dairies, like Hands, with hardly any margin for profit. Dad investigated the possibility of getting financing for setting up a pasteurizing facility, but no one was willing to loan the money when we didn't own the property. It would require a lien on tangible property. Mother and Dad felt the only option was liquidation. Dad was extremely bitter. He knew that had we been able to purchase the other farm we could have found financing for setting up pasteurization and to further expand operations; but, it was not to be.

The best auctioneer in the county was retained to do the sale. Flyers and ads had been sent all over the area including northeastern Colorado. On the day of the sale they came from miles around and even from out of state. We had developed somewhat of a good reputation for having really good milk and we did have a blend of dairy cows that would be desirable for anyone. Apparently that word had gotten out. I remember sitting behind the barn crying as each of the cattle was auctioned off. There goes Old Blackie, and there goes Old Red. Almost all of them had names. And then came the hardest one of all. I heard the auctioneer say, "And now we have this beautiful paint cow pony. I am told she is an excellent cow horse and gentle with children. What am I bid for her and her colt?" Pixie had recently given birth to a foal out of an Arabian stallion. When I heard those words by heart went cold. My crying turned into sobs. It was the saddest day of my young life. I was somewhat consoled by the fact that Ronald Paris had talked his dad into bidding on Pixie and he had been successful; so, Ronald said whenever I wanted to come out and see her, I could.

Our lives now turned in a totally different direction. The proceeds from the sale were sufficient to purchase a house in town. Both Mother and Dad needed to seek employment as well as the rest of us. The house was located on the north side of town on the side of a hill overlooking the city. It was just a few thousand yards below the two huge water towers that sat on top of the hill and provided all the water for Sidney. Dad found employment as the clerk for the Commercial Hotel, Mother became an orderly for the local hospital, John went to work for Farmers Produce, Robert for the lumber yard, and I found my first job selling portable typewriters. Going door to door through the town, I found a typewriter dealer that thought it might work to have a thirteen year old boy hawking his wares. I can't say this was a very successful effort, but I did manage to sell enough typewriters to buy one for myself. That portable Royal typewriter would follow me all the way through high school and college.

Late in my thirteenth year, I was hired by Marvin Anthony, owner of Farmer's Produce. My brother John was already working there. It was a multi-faceted retail shop that bought chickens, turkeys, eggs, and cream from the farmers in the county and then had all the products the farmers needed from town. As I recall, the starting wage was forty-five cents an hour. The farmers would start showing up when the store opened at 8:00 a.m. and there would be a steady flow of business till 5:00 p.m. We would go out and meet their pick-ups and help carry in the cream or eggs and then carry out the bags of feed they would buy. We carried dog food, hog food, grain, and twenty pound bags of flour. In addition to the work we did up front, we had to learn to test cream for butterfat content. That determined what price would be paid the farmer. One of the big jobs was candling eggs. My sister, Alice, had worked several years earlier for one of the other produce companies in town candling eggs and she had taught me how to do four at a time. The candling was to weed out eggs that had blood spots in them. They had to be sorted for size. We learned to recognize if they were small, medium, or large by their look and feel. If there was any question, we had a scale that would tell us. My least favorite job was slaughtering and processing chickens. We had large cooling vats and cleaning tables. The chickens were scalded and then placed on the rotating picker. After they were cleaned, they were packed in ice for shipping. Some went to local restaurants, but most of them were shipped off to restaurants in Wyoming. Each day we would take the company pickup and go to the Union Pacific shipping office with the produce being shipped out. I didn't have a driver's license yet; but, Mother had taught me to drive when I was eight or nine. In those days nobody seemed to pay much attention. All the farm kids drove. It was just an accepted reality. There was no doubt that we were entering a new phase of our family history. From now on, things would be different. I often yearned for a return to what we had before.

3

An Awakening

IT IS EXTREMELY DIFFICULT TO PINPOINT EXACTLY WHEN we first become aware of our spiritual nature, and a sense of knowing that there is something that is more important than ourselves even if we cannot quite identify what it is. When we are born, we are totally selfish babies. All that matters is that our needs be met. We care for nothing beyond ourselves. This is the natural state of life; but, if we follow the normal process of growth and mental development, at some point we begin to realize that we are not the only reality. We are just a part of a much larger whole. It is in our own self-interest to become a cooperating partner in the bigger picture. It is unfortunate when a child cannot get past that first level. I have met adults that still seem to be stuck at the first level.

For me, that awareness came quite young. I cannot account for that apart from the tutelage of my mother and the environment of which I was a part. Even though I cannot pinpoint it, I believe it occurred in my 4rth and 5fth year. I remember sitting in the grove of trees behind our house marveling at the wild flowers, watching the Baltimore Orioles building their nest, just looking at the beautiful sky, chomping down on a crabapple and thinking to myself; how did all of this come to be? It gave me a sense of awe just thinking about it. It is still a mystery to me how anybody of any age can look at our natural world, even if they are uneducated about any of the sciences, and not be awed, and moved to a sense of reverence. This is why, even in the ancient world, they worshiped their pagan Gods.

Mother's Christian faith was always a part of our home even though she and Dad did not attend church. The primary reason was, I am certain, that Sundays were always work days. It was normally the only day that Dad was home and there was always much to be done. The other reason was because Dad had felt burned by some bad experiences with preachers he considered to be charlatans. His experience with grandfather hadn't helped. He also held a deep seated suspicion and disdain for the Catholics which had been passed on to him from his stepfather. Mother was aware of how he felt and as his loyal wife she honored him by simply fulfilling her role as Mother and homemaker. She still had grace at meals and read to us from her family Bible or from a book that had all the Bible stories. We honored all the Christian holidays.

Even though Mother and Dad were not attending church, my sisters, Alice and Dorothy, began attending the First Christian Church in Sidney when they started high school. That is where their school friends attended, and Alice ended up singing in the choir. A few years later, Dorothy followed suit. Alice was able to drive, so she would take the car to go to church. It was while we were still living at that first farm that Alice said to Mother that her brothers needed to be in Sunday School and Mother agreed. I remember the first time we went how impressed I was by everything. My teacher was very nice and I loved the lessons. The large Sallman portrait of Jesus hung on the wall of the classroom. I found it awe inspiring. The pastor, Reverend Gardner, was a large portly man with a booming baritone voice. Both he and his wife were trained musicians. She played the piano for church and he directed the choir. It was thrilling to set there and see my sister in the choir and I began to learn the hymns that would become a part of my life. For reasons I never fully understood, my brothers were not as taken with it as I was. We would all eventually be baptized, but it seemed to me their enthusiasm was different than my own. They would have to speak for themselves, it is not fair for me to make that judgment, but it was my impression.

I had always enjoyed singing. When the school teacher came to call when we first moved to the farm, Mother stood me on an orange crate and asked me to sing the National Anthem for the teacher. I did as I was asked while Mother and Dad proudly watched. Now that interest in music began to show itself at the First Christian Church. I belted out the hymns louder than anyone around me, and people began to take notice. It was not long before they were asking me to do special music in church. It was always just one of the hymns; "In the Garden" or "The Old Rugged Cross" or "Whispering Hope". They were always well received. I can't say for certain when it was, but it must have been when I was nine or ten, I was to do a solo for church and both Alice and Dorothy were in the choir. Mother and Dad showed up in church to hear us. Dad was quite impressed with Reverend Gardner's sermon and both he and Mother began attending church. Ultimately, both Mother and Dad joined the church and began attending regularly.

When I was twelve years old, my brothers and I were baptized. It was at that evening baptismal service that I dedicated my life to Christ. It was a solemn moment for me, and one that has been a part of me ever since. I do remember that I thought Rev. Gardner was going to drown me in the immersion tub, but he lifted me up before I had to breathe. That night had been special for me because I had just turned twelve, and I remembered that Jesus had gone to the temple in Jerusalem when he was twelve years old and when his father found him there and asked him what he was doing he said to his father, "Did you not know that I must be about my Father's business". I felt a sense of kinship with that one whose portrait hung in our class room.

It was right after that when Rev. Gardner's wife offered to give me voice lessons if I would in return mow their lawn once a week. After asking permission, I gratefully accepted. She was a trained voice teacher having graduated with a degree in music. This experience, however, began to raise some questions in my mind about the pastor and Mrs. Gardner. In addition to mowing the lawn, she wanted help in getting some stuff out of the house. They had case after case of empty pop bottles that had just been accumulating in the house. The house looked like it had never been cleaned recently and the pastor was just sitting there in his chair in the middle of that mess like a beached whale. I took my voice lessons, but I began to have serious doubts about the pastor. I had looked up to him as my hero, but no more. My instinct proved to be correct with the events that followed. Dad was always one of those people that went all out when he committed to a job or a project of any kind. He was the same way when he joined the church. When the annual election came up for deacons, Dad was nominated and gladly accepted. The deacons had to be voted on. Dad was rejected. I never knew why, but he was embarrassed and left the church. It had burned him again. At almost the same time, the Board of Elders were meeting to discuss firing Rev. Gardner. It seems that he had for the past several years been embezzling money from the church and that had just been discovered. They chose not to prosecute, but he was reported to his conference and the last we knew of him he was selling cars in Omaha. I stayed on with the church, but my family drifted away. That would not change until I was in high school. That was now just around the corner.

4

My High School Years

HIGH SCHOOL WAS FOR ME A TOTALLY NEW ADVENTURE. It was exciting, but challenging in many new ways. There were a number of the kids from my eighth grade class that were entering with me; but I had not had many friends in that group. I had been the butt of a lot of jokes and teasing in gym class because of my skin and I was clumsy trying to do flips on the matt. Our gym coach was relentless in trying to get us to do flips I would usually end up hitting my forehead with my knee. I had many headaches. Young children of that age tend to make a mountain out of mole hill and I am certain I placed more significance on the gym experience than it deserved. Interestingly enough, even though I resented Coach Leo Shuman almost to the point of hatred, later on he would be my football coach in high school, and he became one of my strongest supporters. I learned to respect him very much.

My freshman year was a very mixed bag. Dealing with the upper classmen was a challenge. There were at least a half dozen bullies that seemed to live for chances to intimidate the smaller kids. I was taking a class in shop where we did wood working and some welding and even some auto mechanic work. Every day in the hall to the workshop there would be one or two of the bullies that would give you a hard bump and then say, "Why are you bumping me?" When you would respond, "I didn't bump you, you bumped me", they would say, "Do you want to make something of it?" all the while putting up their fists. I only weighed about eighty-five pounds at that point and the last thing I wanted to do was fight. Finally, however, it came to that. A person cannot forever abide being intimidated. At the end of the day, we would all come piling out of the school. The bus would be there to take the kids that lived at the Sioux Ordinance Depot. I was always in a hurry because I was working part time for Farmers Produce after school and on weekends. One night coming out the door someone pushed me hard from behind and I fell on the sidewalk. I got up with my skinned knee and looked to see who it was. It was bully number one. He said, "Do you want to make something of it?" Almost without thinking, I swung and hit him in the face knocking him down. He was startled and surprised, but by now a lot of the kids were milling around watching. He outweighed me by at least seventy five pounds. He got up and gave me a sound beating, including a broken nose. I was still on the ground when the principal showed up. The bully, knowing he was probably in trouble had already disappeared down the street. The principal took me into town to Dr. Cook's office and he straightened my nose and bandaged it. I would have two black eyes for a couple of weeks. When Dad learned what had happened, he angrily stormed into the school and confronted the principal and wanted to know how he could allow this behavior on school grounds. I never knew the details of that conversation but, I do know, it was the end of the bullying incidents. Dad could be quite intimidating himself.

During my freshman year, I joined the glee club and also began playing in the band. I did not have an instrument and the only instrument that was provided by the school was the tuba. So, tuba it was. I had one free hour each day to practice and learn. By the time I would graduate, I would be an accomplished player. As a senior, I made all-state and went to Omaha to play with students from all across the state. I remember our big final number was "Rhapsody In Blue". It was played with a world renowned pianist. I can't recall his name. I do remember that my tuba solo for the spring concert was "Billy Blow Hard". I think I still remember the fingering for it till this day. Playing tuba was as they say, "a kick in the head". Mother and Dad came to the concert and Dad laughed his head off. It was a number that would do that to you. I almost immediately became a member of the pep band that would go to all the basketball games. It was a small group, just trombone played by Robert Jewett, Hamilton on clarinet, Chuck Bagby on sax, Billy Burr on baritone, and I can't remember who was on trumpet and drums. Our participation in the games tended to elevate our standing with the other students. On the nights when there was an out of town game, one or two of the parents would haul the pep band. Dad even did in once.

There are no other stand out memories from my freshman year but, that was all to change in my sophomore year. During the summer, a new pastor had been assigned to the Methodist Church in Sidney. His name was Rev. Walter Jewett. He had been serving in the military as a chaplain in Trinidad. He came to Sidney along with his three children, and he would ultimately become the one who changed the direction of my life forever; but I can't get ahead of the story. Walter's oldest son was Robert. Robert was going to be a freshman. We met in school, and Robert started having the same issues I had faced as a freshman. I took him under my wing and tried to help him. We had one class together and were able to help each other with lessons. I found we had so much in common that we soon became the best of friends. The Methodist Church had a recreation room in their basement that included a shuffle board and a ping pong table. On days when I didn't have to work, Robert would invite me to go down to the church and play table tennis after school. It was not long before I discovered that most of the kids I knew were in the Youth Fellowship at the Methodist

Church. My church had virtually none. Among those attending there was John Hardin, the only African American in our school. He had also become a good friend, and he would join us to play ping pong. The result was predictable. I joined the Methodist Church. It had nothing to do with theology or doctrine. It was where the kids were, and I really was taken with Rev. Jewett. He was a bundle of energy. In every way, he seemed the polar opposite of what I had seen in Rev. Gardner. It was my own choice to join the Methodist Church, but I immediately began to tell Dad about Rev. Jewett. I explained that he was an ex- chaplain, and he really knew how to talk to the common people. I said, I really liked his sermons and I think you would too.

Almost immediately, I was asked to join the choir. Miss Crellin, my music teacher in high school, was the choir director at the church. She had started prepping me to sing a solo for district competition, so she was aware that I had a reasonable good voice and what she called perfect pitch. Shortly thereafter, Miss Crellin asked me to do special music for the church service. She gave me the music to learn "The Holy City". When Dad learned that I would be doing a solo in church, wild horses couldn't have kept him away. That Sunday, Mother and Dad were in church. Rev. Jewett was already having an impact on the community and the church was full. I almost didn't see them up in the balcony .Later, dad would tell me how much he enjoyed Rev. Jewett's sermon. The hand writing was on the wall. All the family ended up joining the Methodist Church except John. For some reason, John, we called him Bill, seemed less interested than the others. I have always wondered if his lack of interest was because he felt I received an undue amount of attention from Mother and Dad. Considering all his other issues, that would be understandable, and that possibility has always haunted me.

Over the next year, the bond between Robert Jewett and John Hardin and myself continued to grow stronger. We formed a little cell that included the three of us and a couple of others. We left the door open if others wanted to join us but it was with the understanding that we would be discussing and pondering serious issues. We wanted to study questions like, how do we know there is a God? Where did evil come from? Is there any way to know what heaven is like? Is there a heaven? There were only a few who had any interest. I've often wondered if we were somehow unique or unusual. Perhaps it was just propitious that the three of us found each other and that we had common interests.

One day Rev. Jewett happened in on one of our little cell meetings. We had never told him what we were doing, but he was immediately interested and wanted to give us the benefit of his knowledge. I was, more or less, the leader of the cell, so he handed me a book out of his library. It was one of his text books from Boston Theological Seminary. He said you may find this interesting. I have tried to remember the name of the book, but it was borrowed and returned, and I have never been able to find it. I do remember the first line of the preface. It is etched in my memory. It said, "Theology is the systematic exposition and the rational justification for the intellectual content of religion." I read the book from cover to cover and it became a source book for our cell's pondering.

Our group became more relevant in the summer of my junior year. Rev. Jewett hired a pre-seminary student from Nebraska Wesleyan to be Youth Director for the three summer months. Dean Lanning was an immediate hit with all the kids. He was not only a delight to be around, but his knowledge was a source of envy. He loved to play games and he was very competitive. We all liked that. One of his sports was wrestling and we would set up the mat and take turns trying to beat him. He almost always won. He joined our cell and those three months resulted in a friendship that lasted through the years.

The highlight of the summer was a week spent at summer camp at Camp Comeca in Cozad, Nebraska. Camp Comeca was the Methodist camp for the state of Nebraska. I was able to get a week off from work to attend. The camp was located about ten miles south of Cozad and had all the amenities for a good camp. For me, that week became a powerful reinforcement for the commitment I had already made at my baptism. Each night we would have night watch. The kids were asked to find a spot all alone to pray and meditate or perhaps to write a poem, if so inclined. I found the same spot each night on the highest hill that looked out across the valley. The lights from a distant village could be seen from there and the stars seemed so bright you could almost reach out any grab one. It became an awe inspiring experience. I had been reading the book of collected works by Bishop Sheen, the Catholic Bishop that had been in the news frequently back in the late forties. He was not only a scholar but also a poet of some note. Sitting on that hill brought to my mind his little verse which I had memorized:

> There was a night, there was a hill, there was a moonlit sky;
>
> An upturned face that hardly sensed the night wind blowing by.
>
> There was a voice, no human voice, I heard it clear and still,
>
> And since that night, and since that voice, I've loved each starlit hill.

I heard no voice, or anything that esoteric; but, I definitely felt the power of a connection with something beyond myself. By the end of the week, I had recommitted myself to Christ and told everyone I was going to go to Nebraska Wesleyan University when I graduated, and I was going to study for the ministry.

Christmas of 1948 turned out to be a very difficult time. My dad was suddenly taken ill with severe rectal hemorrhaging. The local doctor did not think he was capable of dealing with it and told us that Dad needed to be taken on an emergency basis to University Hospital in Omaha. I was designated to go with him. The deputy sheriff drove the ambulance and we rode from Sidney to Omaha with red lights on. It was a scary ride at speeds that seemed to me excessive. That was most likely because I had never traveled that fast before. I noticed that the deputy kept taking a little nip out of his thermos. I don't think it was water. We arrived in Omaha in record time and Dad was placed in the hospital. As soon as Dad was settled in, we headed back to Sidney at a much more reasonable speed. By the time I got back, Mother had been able to make the necessary arrangements at home so she could go to Omaha. She took the train to be with Dad and help make any decisions they would have to make. The end result of Dad's treatment was a surgery to remove two or three feet of intestine.

We were approaching the New Year and the Muhrs had planned a New Year's get together at granddads house in Bridgeport. He had retired from the ranch and turned it over to his son Cecil. He and grandmother had purchased a home in Bridgeport. We had planned to attend as a family, but now both Mother and Dad were in Omaha. In a phone call to grandmother, it was decided that Robert, Loren, Buddy, and myself would ride the Burlington Railroad to Bridgeport. She would make room for us to stay overnight and then we could ride the train back to Sidney. John would stay home. He was needed on his job at Farmers Produce. I don't know what the round trip fares were on the Burlington, but they must have been fairly inexpensive. I had reservations about going, but the lure of the New Year's feast that I knew awaited us over-ruled any apprehension. As we expected, it was a sumptuous meal. Much better than we had been cooking for ourselves.

It was late afternoon on January 2nd, 1949, when we boarded the train to return to Sidney. It had started to snow and the temperature had turned very cold. Little did we know that Nebraska was about to experience what has come to be called the blizzard of the century.

The further south we went, the worse the weather. By the time we reached Sidney the drifting was so bad they stopped the train and it would go no further. The Burlington Depot was on the south side of town about a mile from home. The depot was dark as was the entire town. Everyone was hunkered down to ride out the storm. With no other choice, we began the long trek home. The drifts were already nearly chest high in places. Buddy and Loren were having trouble getting through them. Robert was doing yeoman's duty practically carrying Buddy. I was having difficulty myself, but I was trying to help Loren. Somehow we managed to struggle our way through an almost totally dark city and up the last hill to home. When we got there the house was cold and John was huddled under a blanket on the couch trying to keep warm. He had neglected to order fuel for the heating stove. It was already late night. Whatever was to be done would have to wait for morning. We all went to bed huddling under extra blankets for warmth.

The next morning the storm was still raging. The front door to the house was almost totally covered with drifting snow. Robert called the local emergency number, but was told that no immediate help was available and they were uncertain when it would be. To make matters worse, we discovered that the pipes in the kitchen had all frozen overnight, so there was no water. Our kitchen range was electric; but, all the power was out all over the city and we were on candle light, flashlights, and a kerosene lantern. The next two days were just days of making do. We had two gallons of milk on hand for cereal and other stuff for sandwiches. Mother had a stock of canned fruit and tomatoes. Using the heat from our kerosene lantern, Robert was able to melt some snow for drinking water. Fortunately, we did have a small pail of extra kerosene. On the third day an emergency crew brought us fuel and we finally had some heat in the house. That same afternoon Mother arrived back home. She had come back early worried about her family. When she got there, Robert had successfully thawed the pipes and we had water.

The storm of 1949 is still considered to be the worst blizzard in Nebraska history. You can go on line and see the pictures from that storm. An entire train was covered up on the Union Pacific just west of Sidney. Some of the drifts were over thirty feet tall. It would be several weeks before Sidney would fully recover. No one who lived through it will ever forget it. The shepherding that Robert provided for me and my brothers during those difficult days engendered a deep respect for him that lasted till the day he died. He was the man.

When I was a senior, I decided to go out for football. I had grown some. My eighty five pounds was now a strapping 123 pounds. That was small, even for high school standards, but I was scrappy and I tried to make up for my size by being aggressive. Since I had never played football and had no special ball skills, the coach put this little scrapper at defensive right tackle with the mandate to just hit somebody and try to tackle the runner with the ball. I didn't get to play much in the A games, but I reconnected with my old eighth grade coach who was also the high school football coach, Leo Shuman. He noticed my willingness to "get it on" and he seemed to make a special effort to help me. It happened that Coach Shuman was also the Lay Leader for the local Presbyterian Church. Somehow he had become aware of my decision to study for the ministry. One day he came to me and said that their church was going to be celebrating Youth Sunday in two weeks, and they thought it would be nice if I could come and deliver the Sunday message that day. I was flattered and a bit awed by the prospect, but I agreed. So, in the fall of my senior year, I delivered my very first sermon in the Presbyterian Church of Sidney. I selected my scripture from the Gospel of Matthew 7/24-27. "Build Your House Upon The Rock". I think I could almost repeat that sermon today.

I believe part of the reason Coach Shuman had singled me out was because he was aware that I had some ability as a public speaker. In my Junior year, I had won the American Legion's annual speech contest for the best speech on the American Constitution. The first place winner received a twenty-five dollar war bond. By today's standards that would hardly be worth going after but, I didn't do it for awards, I did it for fun. It was a challenge and that was all I needed. My sermon was well received and my Mother was thrilled. My dad was beginning to have misgivings. He thought the decision I was making was premature and unwise. I knew that Dad's dream for me was to fulfill his dream of becoming a professional singer. Dad had a good voice, and he had harbored that secret dream for years. He saw in me the prospect of a future in music. He already had me up there on the Major Bowes Amateur Hour. Besides, preachers don't make any money. Certainly, I loved music and performing, but I questioned that my voice was really professional quality. My vibrato was nothing to write home about and my breath control left a lot to be desired. Some of that could be overcome with training but, the important thing is the talent with which you are born. My talent was in public speaking and my desire was to fulfill the commitment I had already made. The next few years would be ones that Dad went along with reluctantly knowing that Mother was thrilled at what I was doing. I have always respected the fact that Dad, despite his disappointment, was willing to allow Mother her enjoyment of the moment. He had spoken his piece, and he never mentioned it again.

There was some feedback from Alice's husband John Adams. John had returned from the war in Europe with two purple hearts and Captain's stripes. They had moved to Lincoln where John intended to work toward his Masters in Agronomy. He thought I should seek a career as an attorney or any one of the professions. We had all come to have a great deal of respect for John's opinion but, my mind was made up.

My classroom work was nothing spectacular. My grades were always decent maintaining a B average. Yet, I knew that with a little more work and effort it could have been an A average. Part of that was just that I had a lot on my plate. With work and my extra-curricular activities, there were not enough hours in the day. I tried to cram most of my assignments into the one hour study hall we had each day. I was well aware that my sister, Alice, had been Salutatorian and she and Virginia Reiker spent every night and sometimes well into the night on their school work. It was a fact that I was often reminded of by the principal. He had ways of bringing it up without appearing to be critical but, I was content with how I was doing. I enjoyed all my classes except algebra. It was the one I struggled with the most. Part of that was the fact that the algebra teacher, Professor Winn, was probably the driest, lest awe inspiring teacher, I ever had. If you weren't asleep when you went in, you would be asleep by the time you got out. Hard subjects need to be taught by competent teachers. It would have helped. Just as Alice's reputation as Salutatorian was one I had to live down, so it was for Loren when he entered high school. He had to live down my reputation for public speaking, band, and glee club. He did none of those things. His talents were in a totally different direction. He was destined to become an Electrical Engineer working in the NASA program. He would become the one that designed the guidance system for the space probe that landed our space craft on Mars. We are all different. That's just the way it is.

The summer after my Junior year, I was offered a job by a farmer that lived just east of Gurley, Nebraska. He had come into Farmer's Produce regularly and I had become acquainted with him there I think he had been impressed with my work ethic. Whatever his motivation, he said he would offer me top wages to work the summer for him. In addition to board and room, he would pay me top wages. The job would be to drive the tractor doing plowing, and raking, and then during wheat harvest to haul the wheat to the elevator in Gurley. There would be some other small chores, but those were the primary duties. It was much more than I was making at Farmer's Produce. I told him, if he could see his way clear to giving me one week to go to Camp Comeca, I would accept. I was already planning for college and some money was needed saving for that purpose. He agreed and I headed for Gurley.

What a fun summer that was. In addition to a great week at

Camp Comeca, I was thrilled to be back on the farm. Working in the field was hot and dusty work but, it was exhilarating. During the summer, I got the worst sunburn I ever had, and also the best tan but, I enjoyed every single moment of it. When the summer came to an end and I headed back to school, it was with reluctance that I left my little room on the farm. Up till now, most of my earning's from work had gone into the family pot. That was true for all the children. Our work was all for the common pot. This time, almost 100% of my summer wages went in the bank for my college fund. That would be true till the day I graduated.

It was in this time frame that another exciting event occurred. They struck oil. There was a farm family that lived about 20 or 25 miles north of Sidney whose children all attended school in Sidney. Two of them were in high school. They had been the subject of a lot of teasing because they always looked like ragamuffins. Their old clothes had been mended and re-mended with patches for a long time. It was obvious that they did not have much. It was on their farm that the wildcatters from Marathon Oil hit their first well, the Mary Egging # I. In a matter of months, they became millionaires. The kids came into school with nice new clothes and they were the envy of every kid in school.

I had gone back to work at Farmer's Produce and all of the farmers coming in from the north were excited about what was happening. Several of them already had producing wells and speculation was rampant. This new event had played a part in what occurred when we tried to purchase the farm east of town. I have long believed that a lot of people knew that tests had been done to suggest that the possibility of oil existed and that wildcatters were already drilling test wells. Had we known, it would not have made any difference; but, it is an interesting part of our family history. In the next few years the area produced, according to records from the state, over 112 million barrels of oil.

During that year, I had already applied and been accepted to Nebraska Wesleyan University in Lincoln. It is one of the most outstanding Methodist colleges in the nation. They were offering a summer course that could qualify you for becoming an accepted supply pastor in their student pastor program. I was determined to take it. Alice and John were now living in University Place in an apartment directly across the street from the Wesleyan campus. John now had his Masters and was working for the Department of Agriculture as an agronomist. They had offered me free board and room to live with them. It was perfect and they were only half a block from the Methodist Church I would be attending; but, it was not to be.

5

So This Is College

IN JUNE OF 1950 THIS WIDE-EYED, SMALL TOWN, COUNTRY bumpkin stepped onto the campus of Nebraska Wesleyan University for the first time. Its rustic buildings a reminder they had been there serving a community of faith for a long time. Old Main, as we called her, was the primary administrative building housing the chapel and all the music rooms. Chapel was twice a week on Tuesday and Thursday and attendance was required of all students. Over the tenure of my college, I was privileged to hear chapel speakers ranging from famous pastors to senators, governors, and even Presidential candidates. It was something I relished. In my second year, I joined the chapel choir.

What would have been a truly intimidating experience was made less so because my friend, Dean Lanning. As you will remember from a previous chapter, Dean was the Youth Director at the Methodist Church in Sidney. He now became my shadow, leading me through the process of orientation and helping me decide my course load and which subjects to take. Dean was a senior and was Mr. VIP on campus. Name the organization and Dean was most likely the President. That first summer, when there was a free hour or two, we would set up the wrestling mat under the trees on the west lawn of the campus and practice wrestling moves.

My initial euphoria about what I was doing was going to be turned into near panic. As I told you earlier, my sister, Alice, and her husband, John Adams, had graciously given me board and room in their home just across the street from campus. That was free, and it was working out beautifully. I was doing a few of the chores around the house, but my responsibility was minimal and it gave me plenty of time for studies. That was going to change abruptly. John was now working for the Department of Agriculture, and he had just been informed that they were transferring him to Rapid City, South Dakota. That transfer was to be immediate.

My reason for panic was primarily financial. When I enrolled at Wesleyan, I had been given a Hester Scholarship. That was a scholarship for pre-ministerial students. It only paid about one quarter of my tuition. I had used the balance of the money I had saved to pay the rest of the first semester. Now I was faced with the necessity of finding housing and money for food as well as planning for how next semester's tuition would be paid. I think panic would be the appropriate word for what I was feeling. I went to the campus housing office and told them my situation. They referred me to a lady that owned a house directly south of campus. She took in students, room only, and she had one spot still open. The rooms were on the second floor and consisted of two bedrooms, each with two double deck bunk beds; so, she could accommodate eight students. Each bedroom had two study desks. We either had to take turns using them or go to the library which had study pods. The only bathroom required some serious planning and occasional negotiation. But my new landlady was very gracious and agreed to give me my first month's rent in return for some yard work. As time would tell, she was a very special lady who had it in her heart to help as many students as she could. She had installed a telephone in one bedroom upstairs so students would be able to call out, which proved to be very helpful, and I thought at the time was extraordinarily thoughtful of her. However, she would admit to me in a casual conversation many months later that her primary motivation was to keep students from coming downstairs and bugging her to use the phone. I ended up living there for my entire college career.

I now had a place to hang my hat, but I still had to eat. One of the other students was working for a drive-up hamburger parlor on the south end of University Place; which was the suburb of Lincoln where the University was located. I rode the bus down to where it was located and applied for work as a car-hop. I had been told that this was the best option for tips which could increase your wage. Most of the car-hops were girls, which I think was their preference; but, they hired me, and I began on the four to ten shift. My tips were at least equal with what the girls were getting; plus we were allowed to have dinner on the house. They had other things on their menu, but I would have to say, I ate a lot of hamburger. To add to my income, I was able to get a job in the student union coffee shop. There I would work the grill for breakfast and then one hour at lunch time. This got me a free breakfast and a free lunch. The hours in between were class time hours, and any free hours were study time. For now, my food problem and my housing were covered. By the time the second semester would roll around, I had saved enough to cover most of my tuition. The college granted me an extension on the balance until I would be able to cover it.

That first year turned out to be a real struggle. I had successfully completed the summer course as originally planned and had been given my credentials from the Methodist Church as what they called an "Accepted Supply", and also qualified me for the college's student pastor program; but burning the candle at both ends had caused my classroom work to suffer some. I still maintained a respectable B average, but I knew it could be better. My Hester Scholarship required that I maintain at least a B average to keep my scholarship. There were a few places I could have found more time.

For example, I had joined the band and they marched and did half time shows for all the football games. All that required some time. Music was in my blood. It was fun and I felt I deserved it. In my Sophomore year, I would go on tour with the band playing concerts across Nebraska and South Dakota; but after that, I decided I had to concentrate on other priorities and I dropped band. Unfortunately, I forgot to formally inform the administrative office of that decision and my only F in college was the first semester of band in my Junior year. It almost dropped my grade average below the needed B. One of my dumb mistakes.

I must not forget to mention that I was able to cover the balance of my tuition for my second semester of my Freshman year by something else for which Rev. Jewett was responsible. As I will be mentioning later, Rev. Jewett had been elevated to District Superintendent of the Kearney District. As he explained it to me, he was holding an Annual Church Conference at a little church in the Sand Hills of Nebraska. One of the ranchers came up to him and handed him a check. He said, I think there is a student at Wesleyan that is in need of some help. I want you to identify who that is and see that he gets this check. Walter presented me with the check. It was for $500.00. It covered what I owed the school. God knows I had been praying about it. Providential? I think so, and in the letter I sent to that blessed rancher whom I had never met and didn't know, made that point. God does work in mysterious ways.

I told you earlier that I would talk more about Dean Lanning. This is the appropriate place to do that. Dean was President of the Forensics Club and was the team captain for the debate team. He had introduced me to the idea of joining that group. Truthfully, I had never even heard of debate. As I would come to learn, most of the large high schools across the state had debate programs, but I guess Sidney, where less than ten percent of the students went on to college, felt such a program to be unnecessary. Dean told me that he really believed that I needed to get into the debate program. He said the coach was excellent and the speech training I would receive would help prepare me for my intended career. He went on to tell me about a number of famous ministers, such as Harold Bosley, that had been members of the Wesleyan debate squad.

Dean's recommendation was enough for me. I joined the debate team. Here I discovered that most of the Freshmen had come from High School debate programs where they had already learned all the rules and had experienced many debates. There was some catching up to do. This, too, was a compromise on my time schedule, but I came to love it. It fired up my competitive itch. That first year, our Freshman squad went to a tournament in Manhattan Kansas and came home with the tournament title. I was hooked.

In the spring of 1951, as I approached the end of my Freshman year, the District Superintendent of the Lincoln District of the Methodist Church called me and asked if I wanted to be considered for a church assignment. The Annual Conference was set to meet in a few weeks and the Bishop was going to be making selections for the coming year. My response was an immediate yes. My appointment was to the Sprague Community Church in Sprague, Nebraska. So, in June of 1951, just two weeks before my eighteen birthday, I delivered my first sermon in Sprague. This was a farming community and the people were just plain, down to earth, good people. They were accustomed to having young pastors in training and for them it was a mission to be a part of that process. The church was only half full, but the response to that first service was totally positive. The church had a very good pianist and I had arranged to conclude that first sermon by singing "The Lord's Prayer". The damp eyes that met me at the door after the service told me that the message had touched some hearts. My ministry had begun.

After the service, I was invited to dinner with the Lay Leader and his family. What a meal! After eating hamburgers for much of that year, this was like a feast from heaven. She had cooked a beef roast with all the trimmings topped off by delicious homemade pie. They had a large family, all boys, and as we sat at the table and

I was asked to say Grace, a deep sense of gratitude filled my soul. I felt God was being especially kind to me and I resolved that this community of good people would not regret my appointment. Each Sunday, someone was designated to have their young pastor to dinner, and I looked forward to Sunday's for more than one reason.

While having the responsibility of a church meant another restriction on my time, it also meant that I could discontinue my work as a car-hop. It had been very demanding of my time. My church responsibility included directing the choir, which met for practice on Thursday nights, and calling on members in their homes as well as seeking out new members from among the un-churched. Dropping my car-hop job made all that doable. While the income from the church was not large, as I recall it was about $300.00 a month, it more than made up for the car-hop job.

As I entered my Sophomore year, I was joined by my high school friends, Robert Jewett and John Harden incoming Freshmen. They both decided to come live with me. John was on a basketball scholarship that covered his tuition. Robert didn't have one; but, he didn't need one. He was free to pursue his studies without the burden of work. John ended up living there, as I did, for his entire college career. Robert, however, was only there for a portion of the first semester. He decided to pledge to the Phi Tau Fraternity and soon left to live at the Phi Tau House. We wished him well, but I was secretly disappointed that he had chosen one of the Greeks. I understood some of his reasoning. Robert had always been very scholarly. His passion was to be the student with the A+ and the Phi Tau's had the reputation on campus for their seeming ability to turn their members into scholars. They had several Rhodes Scholars to their credit. I was already a member of the Barbarians in the campus organization called the Barbs. It was the largest organization on campus. It was for all those students who chose not to join a Sorority or a Fraternity. John decided to join me in Barbs. I'm not certain, but I suspect, as an African-American, he would not have been welcome in any of the Fraternities. Prejudice was still very much alive in the 1950's. We both remained in Barbs for our entire time at Wesleyan. I was honored to become its President in my senior year.

Early in my Sophomore year, as a part of our forensics class, everyone was asked to prepare an oration on any topic that would relate to a current event that had been in the news. This was done in coordination with other colleges around the state. At that time, Senator Joseph McCarthy was garnering all the headlines with his senate investigations of suspected communists. I knew that Senator McCarthy was a hero to my father, but I believed he was guilty of overreach and that McCarthyism, as it has come to be called, posed a threat to civil liberty. My oration was on that subject. I and one other student were selected to represent Wesleyan in the state contest. Somewhat to my surprise, I won the state title and was then eligible for the national tournament in Chicago at McCormick University. The school administrators told me they did not have enough money in their budget for the Forensics Department to be able to send anyone with me to Chicago; but, they would send me alone. The ride to Chicago on the Union Pacific was an adventure in itself and then navigating getting to and from the University in the big city was an education. In the end, I did not place in the nationals. Fortunately, the tournament was held during the week, so I was able to return in time for my Sunday service. By this time, my father had read a copy of my speech, and he was unhappy with me for a period of time. I guess you could say that I was indicative of the liberalism that always seems to permeate the college campus and my father represented conservatism. That may be true; but, it does not compare with what is occurring on college campuses today.

As my Sophomore year progressed, I was elevated to the number two team on the debate squad. That meant traveling to tournaments further away. Whenever a debate road trip meant being gone on a week end, which was not often, by permission of my church board, I would have a substitute to fill in. Usually, either Bob Jewett or John Harden. I don't remember what our over-all record was for the year, but we did win some tournaments. In my Junior year, I was elevated to the number one spot along with Bob Whited. Bob had been in the military and was several years older. He was a suave, smooth talker that could charm the frost off the pumpkin. What he lacked was the discipline to do any serious research on topics being debated. One of the primary, and maybe the most important, elements in debate was doing adequate research on the topic to have enough ammunition in your card file to be able to counter any anticipated attack by an opponent. Rather than do any research, Bob relied on the work of others on the squad. We all helped each other. But, doing the research gave you a familiarity with the material that you would not have otherwise.

Each year, the National Collegiate Board would select a topic for debate that would be the topic for the entire year. The topic was always stated as an affirmative proposition. This year it was: "Resolved; that the United States should establish a permanent program of price and wage controls". The way it works in debate is you alternate which side of the issue you are on. Now you are for it, now you are against it. One of the outcomes of that exercise is that you usually ended the year with a different personal position than the one you may have started out with. I have often thought that this would be a good exercise for our politicians. If they were forced to look at both sides of every issue, there might be less acrimony between them.

By the end of the year, we had established enough points in the college ranking system to be invited to the regional elimination tournament in Ames, Iowa, to qualify for the National Tournament at West Point in New York. As was our custom, we rode in I-Samuel Duck. I-Samuel Duck was our pet name for the speech wagon that we used for all our trips. It was a three -seated Studebaker wagon that looked almost like a limo. Don't ask me how we named it. I don't remember, but we all had an affection for that vehicle. On this trip we ran into a fierce blizzard about twenty miles east of Omaha. Our debate coach, Walter Murrish, was usually our driver, but he was not real accustomed to driving in snow having been raised in the South, so Bob and I were alternating on the driving. After going into the ditch twice and having to be pulled out with a tow truck, we finally made it to Ames in time for the tournament. There were teams there from all the Midwest States. In the end, Bob and I prevailed and we were on our way to West Point.

We were the first to make it to West Point since Harold Bosley had done it some years before. Only thirty two teams qualified. It would prove to be an exciting adventure. The trip would be planned so there would be enough time to go to Washington, D.C. and visit some of the sights and tour the Whitehouse. A practice debate was scheduled with George Washington University which drew a huge crowd of both students and area adults, and I think a few politicians. From Washington, we drove directly to New York where another practice debate had been scheduled with Brooklyn University. Brooklyn was like culture shock to a Nebraska boy. The Brooklyn accent knocked me out.

We stayed at the YMCA in downtown New York. We had two days there. The first night our coach took us to a famous nightclub in Harlem called "The Cotton Club" with the admonition that this knowledge was not to be shared with the college administrators as they would probably not approve. The ladies in the stage show were beautiful, the music was extraordinary and over-all, it was a night to remember. The next day, after a full schedule of sight -seeing, which included a ride on the Stanton Island Ferry, a visit to the Empire State Building, and a short visit to the Metropolitan Museum, we had reservations at the Waldorf Astoria for dinner and the dinner show. The school was picking up the tab for most of the trip, but we had to stick to a budget for our meals. When we saw the menu at the Waldorf Astoria we all gulped a few times. We were going to have to pick up part of the tab. I settled for ham and pineapple sauce. It was the cheapest thing on the menu, but it was still over twenty-three dollars and then there would be the tip. In the end, we all had a great time. Count Basie was the orchestra providing the music and Lena Horne was the featured performer.

When we left the Waldorf, Coach Murrish took us to one more place that was just a block from the YMCA. It was a bar with taxi-dancers. Now the coach doubled down on our pledge to secrecy. I think he really wanted to give us a peak at life and a culture that would be entirely unfamiliar to us; and, I sensed that he wanted to reward us for a year of hard work and effort. It definitely was a new experience. You bought tickets from the booth. Each ticket was a dime. The girls would do one dance with you for one to three tickets. The coach gave us each ten tickets. When those were gone, a tired student went home to bed. I was not certain if my church would approve of all we did, but in my heart of hearts, I felt we had done nothing for which we needed to feel ashamed. The next morning we were off to West Point.

What a beautiful drive up the Hudson River to West Point. The Northeast has a beauty all its own. It is so totally different than the Midwest. The best word to describe it is to say it is greener. It was the day before the start of the tournament and we were being housed in some of the West Point barracks. Meals were in the regular dining room right along with the cadets. The upper classmen sat together and were served by the Plebes. Those were the Freshmen. One Plebe had been assigned the responsibility of serving us. All the debaters sat in one section, but all were served by Plebes. The food was great, and during the course of the next three days we had opportunity to have some interesting exchanges with some of the cadets. Perhaps the most thrilling part of the visit was watching the cadets in their drill exercises on the drill field and the ceremony with raising and lowering of the flag. Each night ended with the playing of taps.

The tournament itself turned out to be somewhat of a disappointment to us. We came to win, but were only able to pull off a fifth place. That's not bad out of thirty two teams, but it was not what we had envisioned. Holt Spicer, a real stem winder from Redlands University in Redlands, California was selected as outstanding speaker for the tournament and his team won the National Championship. Our coach said he was proud of our performance, but we were still disappointed. When the tournament was over we returned to Lincoln by way of Niagara Falls and Chicago. When we got back, "The Plainsman", our college newspaper, hailed our accomplishment as historic. I guess I didn't share their enthusiasm.

When I got home from New York, my roommate, John Harden had just returned from a basketball tournament in Oklahoma. He had a horror story to tell. He had not been permitted to stay with the team at the hotel. They found a black family in town to put him up in their home. While the team was eating steaks, John was eating chitlins. He was not permitted to use the dressing room or the showers. They put a curtain right on the floor of the basketball court. He had to dress there. Despite the fact that John was high scorer for the tournament, he fouled out in the first half of every game. I was furious. It was my opinion that the coach, who had been raised in the South, should have insisted that John be treated equally or withdraw from the tournament. I had become a contributor to "The Plainsmen" and the next edition carried my scathing and angry response to what had happened. It became a major issue on campus. When all was said and done, the administration pledged that in the future if something like that occurred they would withdraw from any tournament that discriminated against anyone because of ethnic origin.

Toward the end of that Junior year, another event occurred that could have changed my entire life. I had been working very hard at my church and balancing that with everything else that was on my plate. Part of that included a plan I had put together with my church board for one full week of Evangelistic Services to be conducted by guest ministers. It was a part of our push to increase membership and reach the larger community of the un-churched. The week came off as planned, but toward the end of the week, I began to feel ill. I truly had been burning the candle at both ends, and it caught up with me. Following the church service on Sunday, my church people insisted I go to the emergency room at the hospital in Lincoln. The diagnosis was double low-bar pneumonia. A temperature of 105 degrees said I was seriously ill and my condition was life threatening.

During the next few weeks, the outpouring of love from my congregation was like a magic elixir for reaching a full recovery. In addition to all the hospital visits with gifts given in love, there had been a prayer vigil at the church and I learned that the church had been full. Again, I had reason to be grateful to a gracious God who makes his presence known in the actions and caring of his earthly servants. When I got out of the hospital, the mother of my church pianist insisted that I come to their house for my convalescence. In one more week, I was back to my regular routine, more convinced than ever that my mission in life was the one God intended.

The following year would find me in Grand Island, Nebraska. This takes a little explaining. The previous year, Rev. Jewett, who was largely responsible for my decision to enter the ministry, had been elevated to District Superintendent for the Kearney District. His son, Robert, was my best friend and we shared everything. In one of my conversations with Robert, I said that I might have to lay out of school for one year to get caught up on my bills and put together my tuition for my senior year. Robert was one grade behind me and I said, one positive would be that we would then be in the same graduating class. Apparently, Robert relayed that conversation to his dad. In a few days I received a call from Rev. Jewett. He said that he had been conversing with the Bishop and they were looking for someone to go to Grand Island's Trinity Methodist Church as an Associate Pastor and Youth Director. The primary job would be to establish a new church in a suburb of Grand Island where a new high school was under construction. He said, I am confident that Dr. Chubb, pastor of Trinity, would be pleased to have you. Your commitment would be for just one year and it would more than generate enough income for your senior year. He went on to say that Robert had told him what I was considering and it seemed to him that it was providential that they had been discussing, just that week, in their superintendent's meeting with the Bishop, where they could find someone to fit the bill. The Mission and Outreach budget for the conference was limited, so they needed someone who was willing to do a very big job, but for a price the conference along with Trinity could afford. A single student, like myself, would be perfect.

At that time, Trinity Methodist in Grand Island was the largest Methodist Church in the state, and Dr. Chubb was a legendary pastor. He was in demand as a speaker all across the country and his trips were frequent. To even be considered for this assignment was a mind bender. To have a full year under Dr. Chubb's tutelage would not only be an honor, I knew it would provide me with some grounding that would serve my ministry for the rest of my life. It meant I would have to leave my church in Sprague and the great people there that I loved; but, my income there was small, and this would make it possible for me to finish school. I told Rev. Jewett that I was definitely interested if they wanted me. The next week I met with the Bishop and that was followed by an interview with the Board at Trinity. After going through all the job requirements and listening to my presentation, they voted unanimously to hire me. They had a house just two doors down from the church that would be mine if it was acceptable. It was old and run down and the plumbing didn't work; but there were showers and bathroom facilities in the church next door. The church had purchased the house with the thought of eventually expanding with an additional wing. It was just sitting there empty. It would have been entirely unacceptable to any married man with a family. I think that was part of their thinking in wanting to hire a student. It was definitely not ideal, but it was better than what I had lived in on our first farm. That, too, had been old and run-down; but all it had was a long path to a smelly outhouse. Here I had a nice shower and clean bathroom facilities. Be thankful for God's blessings.

Knowing the reason I was taking a year out of school to take this assignment, the Church Board had asked me to agree that I be paid only what I needed to get by. They would hold most of my salary and give it to me in one lump sum at the end of my tenure. This was entirely acceptable to me, and my ministry in Grand Island began in June of 1953. I learned, immediately, that Dr. Chubb ran a very tight ship. He was a sincerely devout and Godly man; but, he was also a highly organized man who was a taskmaster that expected everyone on his team to perform up to his standards. Each week day began at 7:30 with a staff meeting in his office that would conclude with a brief message from him and a ten minute prayer vigil. The meeting included Dr.Chubb, Alan Justad, the Associate Pastor, a retired pastor who managed the church's home visitation program, Jessie Yost, our church secretary who was studying to become a missionary, and myself. At this meeting, the assignments for the day would be handed out. All three of the pastors were required to take turns on hospital visitation. At least one of us had to be at the main hospital and the Veterans Hospital every day. Dr. Chubb considered this to be one of the most important parts of our ministry.

Each Sunday, the church had three services. The eight-thirty service was usually conducted by Alan Justad, Dr. Chubb always did the eleven o'clock service and we shared the evening service. I was also responsible for the Youth Fellowship. We would hold our meetings prior to the evening service. However, my primary mandate was to start a new church and I had been given free rein as to how that was to happen. I had been told that the Board of Missions was prepared to invest $50,000.00 in a property for the church as soon as we could identify an acceptable location. That became my first priority. I drove every block in the northwest section of town. Finally, I located one that fit the bill. It was an old house sitting on an oversized lot with an empty lot next door. It was just three blocks from the site of the new high school. I gave the particulars on the property to the realtor, who was a member of the board at Trinity and took care of their needs. He said he would quietly find out if the property might be available for purchase. He did and it was. The Board of Missions picked up the tab for the purchase and step one was complete.

You can't have a church without a congregation, so this began step two. Starting as early as June, I began systematically to visit every home in the northwest section of town. At each door, I would introduce myself and explain that we were preparing to build a new Methodist Church in the area. The exact location is yet to be determined; but, I am simply seeking to find out if you would find it welcome, and is it a project that you might enjoy sharing? Anyone that gave anything resembling a positive response ended up in my card file for a later follow-up. In the process of doing this, I knocked on one door that turned out to be the exact right door. The man that answered the doorbell was Richard Tucker. When I explained who I was, he immediately invited me in. He said that he occasionally attended church at Trinity but would prefer something closer to home, and he thought our project sounded exciting. Further discussion revealed that he was a conductor on the Union Pacific Railroad. He was headquartered there in Grand Island. Richard became chairman of my organizing committee.

By the end of summer, through my efforts, and with the help of several others I recruited from the neighborhood, we had created enough interest that we thought we were ready for a church organizational meeting. Several thousand flyers were printed up with my picture and an announcement of the organizational meeting. My Youth Fellowship group from Trinity accepted the challenge of seeing the flyers were distributed to every door in the area. When the night came for the meeting, we were gratified to have close to one hundred in attendance. The attorney for Trinity was there to explain the process of incorporation and answer any legal questions. At this time we were able to disclose the location for the new church. At this meeting we sat up a building committee, an outreach committee, and a temporary Official Board. They would serve until the church became a reality. We were on our way.

There was much work that needed to be done and we were starting with practically zero capitol. Some walls would need to be torn out with some re-enforcement timbers being added for safety to create room for the sanctuary. The roof needed to be replaced. Extra rooms in the house needed to be turned into classrooms for Sunday School. Everything needed painting and we needed to create a worship center and altar. Richard Tucker became my go to guy. Working with volunteers recruited by the building committee we began the process of restoration. We had no general contractor. We were the general contractors. Some of the volunteers were carpenters. Some had done some painting. I don't know if any of us had ever put on a roof. There is a picture of me someplace, pounding shingle nails on the roof. Trinity church pitched in with some donations for materials. They also provided us with a pulpit which they had and some addition items for our worship center. A lot of the materials came from lumber yards in town that donated it to us. I know that was true of the shingles. One of the volunteers had the equipment to clean up the lot to create a gravel parking lot. By late October, the volunteers were able to erect a wooden cross to place on the front of the church along with a sign that read "Home of the new Westlawn Methodist Church", a name that had been chosen at the organizational meeting. The lawyers had needed a name for the incorporation papers. We were done in time to be able to hold our first service in our new church for Thanksgiving. From that time forward, my Sunday mornings were devoted to Westlawn. I continued my work with the Youth Fellowship and the evening worship service at Trinity. My weekdays remained much the same. The morning staff meeting, the hospital calls, etc. The only real difference was that Dr. Chubb always wanted a blow by blow description of what was happening at Westlawn. On any given Sunday, it was kind of a competition to see which church took in the most new members that week. Dr. Chubb, despite his celebrity, was out every week calling on prospective members. He considered it his most important function. In Nebraska, his evangelistic zeal was legendary. Most of my work time was spent making calls on original members of Westlawn, and seeking to evangelize others. Dr. Chubb was my example.

One of my fondest memories of that time was the humor everyone found in the fact that during church, whenever one of the children needed to use the bathroom, they needed to walk right past the pulpit to get to it; and when they were done everyone would hear the toilet flush. There was a general feeling that we were all a part of something special. We were growing rapidly and almost every Sunday we had baptisms to do, or new members to welcome. By the time spring would arrive and I was nearing the end of my time there, the church had grown sufficiently to be able to support a full time minister. At the Annual Conference the Bishop appointed Stanley Ganzel as the first pastor of Westlawn Methodist Church. Stanley had been a senior at Wesleyan when I was a freshman. He had just graduated from seminary. We knew each other, so I was able to help orient him to his new task which was going to be to build the permanent church building. Leaving a church where you have come to love the people is always the hardest part, even if you knew going in that this was the way it was going to be; but, I went back to Wesleyan with a grateful heart and also a new assignment.

Rev. Jewett had completed his time as District Superintendent and the Bishop had appointed him pastor of Centenary Methodist Church in Beatrice, Nebraska. Walter asked if I would accept an appointment as Associate Pastor to him at Centenary. He knew it would be for only one year, then I would graduate and go on to seminary; but, he wanted me to come. I gratefully accepted. That summer was a delight. Robert was at home for the summer, so we had time to get reacquainted and renew our in depth discussions on theology. Again, I was responsible for the Youth Fellowship which included two trips to Camp Comeca; one with the Junior Fellowship and one with the Senior Fellowship. I drove the bus the church owned. My first experience driving a bus.

When I re-entered Wesleyan for my senior year, it was with the blessing of Rev. Jewett that I go out again for debate. He believed it would hone my skills for the pulpit and he heartily endorsed it. Bob Whited had graduated. His team had tried to repeat what happened in '53 but had been eliminated before getting to the Districts. I was, somewhat automatically, given the top spot and my partner would be Melvin Swenk. Melvin was a real firebrand. He had somewhat of a squeaky voice, but he made up for it with his manner of delivery. His arms and hands were in constant motion as he made his points. He was a meticulous researcher and he knew every facet of his subject. The National Collegiate Board had selected for the debate topic for '55 "Resolved: that the United States of America should grant diplomatic recognition to the Communist Government of China". This was at a time when this was a highly controversial subject.

In the late fall, Melvin and I advanced to the Grand National Tournament in St. Paul, Minnesota at St. Thomas University. I don't recall all the teams that were there, but I remember Notre Dame and the University of Kansas which were both always debate powerhouses. In the end, Melvin and I were able to prevail and bring the McClelmele Trophy back to Wesleyan. It looked as big as me. It was presented to us by the mayor of St.Paul. When we got home, that picture was on the front page of "The Plainsman".

In the spring, we once again began the eliminations for the West Point Tournament. The organizers of the St.Paul Tournament considered their tournament to be the national championship, but the National Collegiate Board had always considered the West Point Tournament to be the one to decide the true national champion. Melvin and I were again successful in winning the regional title and advancing to West Point. So, again in l955 I found myself riding I-Samuel Duck up the Hudson River to West Point.

Everything seemed familiar, but the excitement was the same; however this year was going to be different. The topic for debate had been so controversial that the military academies had been forbidden to participate. It would have meant they would have to argue the affirmative side of the issue in direct contravention of current national policy. They were still hosting the tournament and doing everything as usual; but, they were not participating in the competition.

Melvin and I sailed through the preliminaries winning every debate; but, then came the Quarter Finals. Our opponent was the University of Alabama. In the elimination rounds, we drew to see who would be on the affirmative and who would be on the negative. We drew the affirmative. The team from Alabama was very smooth, but most of what they did was what we called in debate "flag waving". It was a call to patriotism with little factual material. There were seven judges. We lost five to two. We learned later that the two votes for us were both debate coaches. The five votes against were all officers from West Point. Alabama was fortunate enough to draw the negative for both of their last two debates and they were crowned national champions for 1955. I was selected as outstanding speaker for the tournament. In an interesting side note, Nebraska Wesleyan University recently presented me with a plague honoring me for leading Wesleyan to the Nationals twice, in 1953 and 1955. Wesleyan has not been back there since 1955.

As I approached the end of my senior year, I was once again faced with the need for additional funds for seminary. Again, Rev. Jewett had a suggestion. He said, I think the good folks at Centenary would enjoy it if you could put on a concert. It could be a fund raiser and I think it would be well attended. The idea appealed to me as music had been a big part of my ministry. I recruited Jay Newberry who had sang with me in the opera at Wesleyan, and several others from Wesleyan. They were all to be paid for their performances. We did a two hour concert which included everything from Broadway show tunes to gospel and even some opera. The house was packed and the offering covered all the costs with enough left over to cover my tuition. You can begin to understand how important Rev. Jewett was in my life.

This chapter would not be complete without mentioning the other activities I participated in at Wesleyan. No doubt, the most important thing about college is the course of study and the learning associated with it. After all, it is the education that we are seeking; however, there is not much to talk about when you are telling about your history class or your psychology workshop. The things we tend to remember are the other things we did in college. When I was a Freshman, I had attended the Wesleyan performance of the opera "La Boheme". I was entranced. The only thing I knew about opera was that my father had told me that opera was just a bunch of fat ladies screeching. To actually see such a marvelous performance opened my eyes to an entire new world of music. Opera is the only art form that combines all three of the dramatic arts: drama, dance, and music. In my senior year, I would be tapped to play the role of the doctor in the first American amateur production of "Der Rosen Cavalier". This extremely difficult Strauss opera had not been attempted by anyone else; but, Wesleyan pulled it off with rave notices from the critics. My role was not a lead role, but it was extremely satisfying anyway.

In my Sophomore year, I had a leading role as the chef in the Drama Department's presentation of the play "Mrs. McThing". In that same year, I took a one semester class in radio and television. That resulted in our class producing a one hour television special called "This Is College" which aired on local Lincoln television. I was the announcer and M.C. It was a fun project. In my Sophomore year, I was president of the Square Dance Club, one of the other fun groups on campus. For two years, I was also Student Union Manager. This simply meant doing clean up at the end of the day and locking up the building. As I write about all these things now, I wonder how it all got done.

Graduation day finally arrived. Both mother and dad were

there for the occasion. They had decided to leave Sidney and move to Denver where Dorothy was working and living. She had started to have her Grand Mal seizures again and while at a theatre in Denver she had one of her attacks and someone had stolen her purse and all her money. They felt they were needed and there was no longer any reason to remain in Sidney. In addition to Dorothy's problem, my brother, Robert, was having problems of his own. He had been on the top of the list for the draft into the Korean War. Rather than wait to be drafted he had joined the Marines. He was stationed at Camp Pendleton in California. He did fine on all the training until he got to hand to hand combat with the bayonet. He did not believe he would be able to kill another human being while looking him in the eye. I could relate to that as well. Mother and dad had found a quick buyer for the house in Sidney and they had everything with them except what they had shipped to Denver to be stored until they arrived there. The plan was to attend my graduation, then go on to California and counsel with Robert and then go back to Denver and find a place there. They had my younger brothers, Loren and Buddy, with them so they all were able to celebrate the day with me. They were only there for one night, and then on to California.

It would be appropriate for me to mention at this point that I never served in the military. All of my brothers did except John. Robert was in the Marines and served in the Korean War. Loren was Navy and Buddy served in the Army. I was subject to the draft; however, I had a draft status of 4D. That status was due to my attendance in college. It put me at the bottom of the list in Cheyenne County. I was never called and I didn't volunteer. It had nothing to do with my feeling or attitude about the military, it was just that my mind was someplace else and my focus was on that.

With college completed, my attention turned to graduate school. I had decided to attend Garrett Biblical Institute in Evanston, Illinois. It had been a part of Northwestern University at one time, but had become a separate entity, even though it was right on the Northwestern University campus just across from their huge library. Garrett was having a summer session that included an advanced workshop on pastoral counseling. Rev. Jewett felt he needed some additional help in that area since pastoral counseling had become such a big part of his ministry. We decided that we would both attend the summer session together. Walter arranged for substitutes for the time he was going to be gone, and we went to Chicago together. My enrollment was for the entire summer. Walters was just for three weeks. I was given a room in the dorm with bunk beds; so Walter was able to stay with me for his three weeks. He got the bottom bunk. I revered this man and it was a pure joy to spend three weeks studying together.

As soon as Walter went home, I began to look for additional sources of income. My search turned up a job at Piser Memorial Chapel, the largest Jewish funeral parlor in Chicago. They had three locations. The one at Foster and Broadway in North Chicago needed a night person to answer the phone and go on pick-ups as needed. They provided a nice little furnished apartment in the upstairs of the mortuary. It seemed ideal to me. It would give me an insight into the customs and traditions of the Jewish Community and when the phone wasn't ringing, it was a quiet environment in which to study. I left my room in the dorm and moved in immediately. It would mean riding the El each day to Evanston, but that was kind of fun.

My learning experience began almost immediately. One of the requirements was to usher for funeral services and wakes that were held in the facility. In my first few days, there was a large wake for a man who had been prominent in town. It was huge wake. They had hired several professional criers. This was a totally new experience for me. I discovered that in the Jewish Community they used professional criers at the wakes. They would surround the casket and weep and wail like Banshee's. This would evoke that same response from members of the family. As I would learn in my classes on dealing with grief, this process greatly enhanced the healing from grief. It was one of many lessons I learned there.

When I first arrived in Chicago, I began church hopping on Sunday to see how services were conducted in each. Most of the time it was Evanston Methodist Church; a very formal church with ushers wearing tuxedos with ties and tails. The Sunday after starting work at Pisers, I decided to attend church at the Chicago Temple. It was the largest Methodist Church in Chicago located right downtown with their tower hovering above the city. The ground floor was the church along with the first two floors of offices and classrooms. The next twenty stories, or so, was office space that was rented out by the church. Above that was the tower and the great steeple and bell. The top floor was the parsonage for the pastor. What an impressive edifice. At that service, the bulletin had a little notice that the church was seeking a baritone soloist for the choir. At the conclusion of the service, I sought out the choir director and asked for an audition. They ended up hiring me. They were doing a radio broadcast each Sunday and this always included special music. The only four members of the choir that were paid was the quartet: a soprano, a tenor, a baritone, and a bass.

There is much more that could be covered about my college years and my entrance into Garrett; but, the challenge is to figure out what to put in and what to leave out. There is no way to cover it without it becoming quite self-centered. Since it's my story and relates my experience, perhaps I can be forgiven for that. I will pick up the continuing story in the next chapter.

6

Look Before You Leap

MY LIFE WAS ABOUT TO BECOME MUCH MORE complicated. After Walter went back home to Nebraska, I felt very much alone; and, yes, a little lonely. I had met a number of other students, but no one that was anything more than a casual acquaintance. My good friend, Robert Jewett, had enrolled at the University of Chicago. He had taken three years of German in college and had his mind set on doing graduate study in Germany. Much of the important theological thought and study was done in German and most of that material has never been translated. It was Robert's plan to learn German well enough to be able to use the original sources for his future work. His was the mindset of a scholar with no notion of becoming a pastor. Since the University of Chicago and Garrett were on opposite sides of the city our opportunities to get together were rare. I believe my feeling of loneliness contributed to the events that would follow.

There was a Swedish restaurant just a few blocks from Piser Memorial Chapel that was my favorite place for a meal or just a pastry treat. It was located right across the street from the old Ford Theatre where John Dillinger had been shot by the FBI. It was while visiting that historical site that I had discovered this marvelous restaurant. Sometime in July I was having a meal there when I saw a poster in the window. It was advertising for all kinds of talent for a show called "Your Big Break". The auditions to be held in various clubs around town. More out of curiosity than anything, I called the number. The man who answered was Mr. Anthony DonGarra. He explained that he currently had a television show airing on WGN called "Little Stars". It was a show for talented youngsters from the age of 6 to 17; but, the plan was in the works for a second show for those 18 and over that were looking for their big break. He went on to explain that he was developing a reservoir of talent for the show by having talent contests in three different clubs in town on Tuesday, Thursday and Sunday. The best talent would end up on his show. I told him that I was not really looking for a big break as I had other career plans; but, I saw your ad and was just curious. When he sensed I was going to end the conversation, he said "Wait a minute, just what is your talent. What do you do?" I said what talent I have is singing. I am the baritone soloist for the Chicago Temple. He said that he needed more talent for his nightclub shows and even if I wasn't looking for a career in music, it would be a good opportunity to make some extra money. They determined winners by audience applause with the winner receiving $25.00 and the runner up $15.00. That won't sound like much to my readers; but you are living in a different age. Back then, that meant a lot of meals. I started going to the shows on all three nights.

Mr. DonGarra had a good thing going. I don't know what the clubs were paying him, but it was a good concept. Tuesday and Thursday were both slow nights for a club. Having this show created enough interest to get a large early crowd into the bar. The prelims would be at 7:00 followed by the finals at 9:00. Just in time for me to get back to Piser for my night shift. Tuesday was the Northside Bar and Grill which was just a few blocks north of Piser. Thursday was Club Odo's, which was on the Westside. Sunday was an afternoon show at the Brass Rail, a locally famous bar right downtown. The piano player for all the singers was a blind musician we called Sachs. He was truly extraordinary. He could play anything. His accompaniment was the best I had ever had. Over the next few months we would do a lot of different types of music; but I soon learned that my best response always seemed to come from my two staples, "Danny Boy" and "Old Man River". Most of the singers were doing strictly pop music; stuff the audiences had heard over and over. But, somehow, the patrons seemed to relate to "Danny Boy", especially those who had started drinking early, and they also liked the bombastic nature of "Old Man River". I started winning shows on a regular basis.

Soon after starting the shows, it must have become apparent to Mr. DonGarra that I was kind of a strange duck in an unfamiliar environment. The only clubs I had ever been in were the ones in New York with my debate coach. I didn't smoke and I didn't drink. When getting to the club, I would find a table somewhere in the back of the room where I would sip a coke or seven-up. Usually, I would have a book or two with me so I could study while awaiting my turn to perform. If I lost out in the prelims, I would head home immediately. If I was in the finals, I would stay only long enough to collect my money and leave. This behavior caught the attention of Mr. DonGarra. I had only met him briefly and any conversation I had with him was just what he needed for his introductions. He was, in fact, rather intimidating. He was a very intense Italian who always looked like he was a little angry about something. As I would later learn, he was a graduate from the Julliard School of Music. His career had included being the lead violinist for the Freddy Martin Orchestra and finally Concert Master for the Chicago Symphony. He had a two hour classical music show every night on FM radio. They were all taped in advance. He was also the lead advertising agent for Advertising Company of America, one of the leading agencies in Chicago. All this in addition to his club shows and his television show. He was a very busy man. I guess he had reason to be intense. In any case, one night after the prelims when we were waiting for the finals, he came over to my table and sat down. He said, I think we need to get a little better acquainted. He commented on my behavior and asked me what I did. I explained that I was a student at Garrett studying to become a minister. He was immediately interested. As he explained, he lived in Evanston and was a member of the Evanston Methodist Church. In fact, he was not only a member, he was one of those ushers I had seen in ties and tails at church. Before the conversation was over, he said, I would like you to meet my family. Would you care to join us for breakfast next Sunday and then we could go to church together and then down to the Brass Rail for the show? I was quick to say yes.

This began an odyssey that would forever change the course of my life. On that first day I met Mr. DonGarra's wife, Virginia. She was charming and a talent in her own right. She was the script writer and talent coordinator for "Little Stars" and had a show of her own on radio called "Listen to Pepe". I also met their daughter, also called Virginia, who immediately attracted my attention. She was not only pretty, she seemed a little demure and somewhat mysterious. Years later, I would come to believe that this entire episode was designed by Mr. DonGarra in order for me to meet his stepdaughter. If he was playing match maker, it worked. Virginia became my very first serious relationship. It may seem strange to some, but I had never had any romances in my life up till that point. Yes, I had dated in college; but, it was usually just one date for a special occasion or a dance. It seemed I was always too busy to be able to devote much time to a social life. My roommates in college had all been very much into the campus social scene, and it always seemed appropriate to align myself with them. As a result, I had the reputation on campus of being a bit of a lothario. Nothing could be further from the truth; but, I had allowed it to happen.

The relationship with Virginia continued to develop over the next few months. I admit to being a little bit star struck by the DonGarra's and their circle of friends. Perhaps the best example of that would be our trip to the "Pump Club". Virginia and I had been going to the tapings of their "Little Stars" show and helping out with props and whatever else needed doing. It was exciting. Over the course of the fall we had met a number of big stars who were appearing as guests on the show. One day after the taping of a Quarter Finals show, Mr. DonGarra said, come on everybody, I'm going to take you all to dinner at the "Pump Club". At that time, it was the ritziest and most fashionable nightclub in Chicago. He had obviously made reservations in advance, because when we walked in we were treated like royalty. A table for four right close to the stage. After a great meal, we settled back to wait for the show to begin. A man came up to the table and began to talk to Mr. DonGarra. He turned out to be Herb Kupsinet, the entertainment columnist for the Chicago Tribune. He had written a column that week on "Little Stars". Mr. Kupsinet said, there's a couple of people in the house I would like you to meet. They would be excellent guests for one of your shows. The waiter brought an extra table and combined it with ours. The two he had in mind turned out to be Elizabeth Taylor and her new husband Michael Todd. They talked about some of the projects they were working on, and the possible future appearance on "Little Stars". I, mostly, sat and listened without contributing much to the conversation. To say I was impressed would be a definite understatement. It was, for me, a memorable event. The noose was drawing tighter.

Finally, the inevitable occurred with my first sexual encounter. When I allowed that to happen, in my heart and mind, we were already married. No proposal had yet been made, but the thought was there. The first thing I did was to go visit my counselor at Garrett. He was also the head of the Psychology Department for the school. I told him everything that had happened and said I was considering a proposal of marriage. His response did not surprise me very much. The things he said were some of the same things that had occurred to me. He said that we came from two entirely different worlds. She had been through the trauma of two failed marriages. She had been abandoned by her father. There had been much trauma at before finding the stability of her new stepdad. Her years of growing up were polar opposites of mine. She had been raised on the streets of New York where her mother was a Conover model; the largest modeling agency in New York. You are a farm boy, he said, with values that are likely much different than her own. In addition to that, she has only a high school education. She will most likely feel intimidated by the educational difference. As he was saying it, I was thinking of my sister Alice who had only a high school education and still helped John Adams to achieve his Doctorate in Agronomy. I said, don't you think that if two people love each other this alone can overcome all the other obstacles we may encounter. He replied, we would all like to believe that is true, but, Rex, I think you are looking at it through rose colored glasses. You are going to end up doing whatever you want to do; but, you have heard my opinion.

When you are young and lonely, and have found someone who says they love you, it is easy to rationalize all the rest. The proposal came with hasty acceptance. The DonGarra's seemed delighted and immediately began preparations for a big wedding at Evanston Methodist Church. Robert Jewett agreed to be my best man. The wedding was a gala affair. Mr. DonGarra played a violin solo from one of the classics and the chapel was full of people I did not know. The same at the reception that followed. What was missing was my family. None of those I loved were there. This primarily for financial reasons. For any of them to travel to Chicago would have been a significant burden. I had already made up my mind that I would have to drop out of Garrett for at least one semester. I reasoned that if I was going to do that, I should take Virginia back to Colorado to meet my family, get a job there, and return to Garrett when I could. The day after the wedding, we were on the train headed to Colorado.

After a brief four day honeymoon in Manitou Springs, we returned to Denver and stayed temporarily with Mother and Dad. They had a spare room. It was only days before I found employment working for the Foss Drug Company in Golden. They had a complete grill and restaurant as a part of their drug store. We found a little apartment on the lower level of a private home and I went to work as a grill cook. This was something I had done in college, so it was not all new. What was new was learning to do steaks and seafood entrees. For this, the owner was an accomplished teacher. It was not long before I had learned to do the pastries, bake bread, and prepare the roasts and turkeys. The School of Mines in Golden had several hundred foreign students, and they all loved homemade bread. They would come in and order two or three servings of bread. We baked every day.

I found myself enjoying what I was doing. It was rewarding. It was good to be near my family. My brother, Robert, had gone to school after getting out of the Marines, to become a body and fender man. He had a good job right there in Golden working for an auto dealership. He also drove the wrecker on the night shift picking up wrecks in the canyons west of Golden. He and his new wife, Janet, a surgery nurse, attended the Methodist Church in Golden. Attending church with them was like coming home. For the first time, it seemed like I belonged but, this was not to last.

Almost immediately, Virginia became restless and started pushing for us to return to Chicago. I knew she was bored. My job started early in the morning and I usually worked a double shift. My urgings for her to find some type of employment that would keep her busy went unanswered. There was always some excuse that made that impossible. The truth was, no effort was made. In the end, I agreed that we would go back to Chicago and perhaps I could get back into Garrett sooner than I expected assuming I could find good employment in Chicago. After confirming with the DonGarra's that they could put us up until I found work, we were on the train back to Chicago.

The first day back, I was successful in finding a job. It was not what I was looking for, but it would work as an interim job. I would be selling cars for the Nash-Rambler dealership in North Chicago.

When I received my first commission check, we rented a furnished apartment close to the elevated train that ran into the city. Since I had no car, it needed to be within walking distance. Selling cars was actually kind of fun, and after listening to the sales pitch of our sales manager, I was beginning to believe that the Rambler was a really good automobile. That opinion was tempered when I heard him tell one of the other salesmen that he wouldn't be caught dead driving a Rambler. My first real taste of hypocrisy. Fortunately, my tenure selling cars would only temporary. I had been circulating my resume in Chicago. That search turned up a very interesting offer. The largest employment agency in Chicago had an opening for a manager of their administrative division. They had their agency set up with divisions. Engineering and Technical Sciences, Sales, Bookkeeping and Office Skills, and Management and Administrative. They did not handle day labor or low skill jobs. The job carried a very good fixed salary plus bonuses and commissions that were performance based. It also provided health insurance. When they agreed to hire me, I was ecstatic. This would mean I would most likely be able to return to Garrett sooner than expected; perhaps not as a full time student, but I had been told of some other options. Meanwhile, I began urging Virginia to search for employment, any kind of employment to keep herself busy. Preferably, something that would be fun that she could enjoy. I don't think she ever looked.

Each day I would ride the El into downtown Chicago. There was an exit very close to my work on Broadway Street. The work was hard, but very rewarding. I found myself interviewing managers for major corporations whose credentials were far more impressive than my own but, my rate of success, early on, had impressed management. My spot was secure but, that, too, was going to end almost before it had opportunity to really get started. The DonGarra's had been following my progress and were pleased with what was happening. They arranged with Virginia to have a surprise birthday party for me at our apartment. They had invited just a small group of their mutual friends. I was, indeed, surprised. A good time was had by all.

The next day I went to work as usual. When I came home the apartment was dark and Virginia was gone. The table still had a few pieces of stale birthday cake that had not been put away. Calls to all her friends turned up no sign. I called the DonGarra's and they came over, but they had no answers. This began a three day vigil with no answers. On the third day, I called the FBI and declared her a missing person. Within twenty-four hours they had located her. Apparently, while I was at work, she had been cavorting with a boy she knew from high school. His father owned a large insurance company in Chicago and their mansion in Evanston had an Olympic size swimming pool and all the accoutrements of wealth. The FBI had been able to learn almost immediately from Virginia's friends what she had been doing. They would not tell me when I called but, when confronted by the FBI and threatened with prosecution they spilled the beans. The two of them had run off to Florida in his fancy sports car and all his money. He had dazzled her with all he could offer. The FBI gave us all the information including the number in Coral Gables Florida where she could be reached. They also gave us the name of the family in Evanston and their address. The agent in charge gave me some very sobering advice. He said, he had been working these kinds of cases for many years. He went on to say, Rex, you may not realize it yet, but your marriage is over.

As soon as the FBI left, Mrs. DonGarra and I went directly to the address they had given us in Evanston. When confronted, the mother admitted that she had seen Virginia at the house on a regular basis and had served the two of them lunch together but, she had no idea this was in the offing. She was very apologetic, but that did little to diminish the pain I was feeling. She said, I think you and Virginia's mother should fly to Coral Gables and see the two of them and see how this can best be resolved. I will gladly pay for the trip. As much as I hated taking her money, I was anxious to confront Virginia myself. We agreed, and the two of us booked passage to Coral Gables.

Unbeknown to us, as soon as we left, his mother booked a private aircraft to fly to Florida to get there ahead of us. The FBI had told her that her son was facing possible prosecution. She flew to Florida, met her son and put him on a plane to Nassau beyond the reach of the FBI. Virginia's white knight in shining armor had turned into a pumpkin. When we landed at the airport, Virginia was at the terminal awaiting us. What followed was a series of conversations with the FBI in Florida along with the three of us. His mother had already flown back to Chicago. Those conversations brought out a new fact. Virginia was pregnant with my child. She had not told her boyfriend and she hadn't told me, but that changed the entire equation. If I abandon Virginia, I will also be abandoning my child. She begged to come home, promising to do better. I relented.

The work at the agency continued with some increasing success. They had graciously given me some time off for my family emergency. The owner had been very empathetic relating to me something similar that had happened in his life. For some time it seemed the ship was going to right itself. But, again it was only a matter of weeks before Virginia was lobbying to move somewhere, anywhere away from Chicago. Her friends there had been very critical and she felt she had to get away. My reasoning that I had a good job and it was going to make it possible to go back to school kept falling on deaf ears. The complaining was continual. One day I learned that Virginia had been talking to her mother's sister, who lived in White Plains, New York. Their daughter and Virginia had been good friends when she lived in New York. They had told her, if you and Rex want to come to New York and find work here, we would be happy to have you as our guest until you can get settled. At first, it seemed like an entirely preposterous idea. It would mean abandoning the idea of returning to Garrett. I knew there were some equally good schools in the east. My friend, John Harden was attending seminary at Drew University. My friend, Dean Lanning had graduated from there, and there were a host of others. Yet, I was very reluctant to leave what I had building in Chicago. In the end, this woos relented again. I had purchased an automobile, so this time we were able to drive. Everything we owned was fit into that automobile. One of the hardest things I had ever done was resigning my job. They had been good to me and given me every break. The owner again was empathetic and promised me a good reference if it was needed.

We arrived in White Plains, and one day later I went into the city to begin my job hunt. Almost magically, that first day lead me to an agency on the fifth floor of the building that housed NBC at number twelve Rockefeller Plaza. The front door of the agency read, Amy Lorton McKay, Management Consultants. I had read a little squib in the Wall Street Journal that Amy Lorton McKay was looking to add someone to her staff. It was not a want ad, but it was a lead. It was strictly a cold call. When the receptionist led me into Mrs. McKay's office I was confronted by a very severe looking woman which told me right away she was all business. When, she asked what I wanted, I handed her my resume and explained we had just arrived in New York, and I needed to find immediate employment. I said, I read in the Wall Street Journal that you might be adding to your staff. She seemed impressed that I had been reading the Wall Street Journal. She looked over my resume and then said, I see you are listing this agency in Chicago as a reference. I have had some dealings with their owner in the past. Would you mind sitting in the waiting room while I give them a call. I sat, apprehensively, in the waiting room looking out the window. Down below was the flags of the nations and the skating rink which was now full of skaters. My thoughts went back to my youth and I thought this is a very long way from that little farm in Nebraska. In about ten minutes, Mrs. McKay called me back into her office. She said that was definitely a good reference. When can you start? I said, when do you want me to start? She said, tomorrow at 8:00 o'clock.

In one day, a new job with increased pay. When I got back to White Plains, Beth and Chuck, our hosts could hardly believe it. Chuck was an accountant with Standard Oil, and he traveled the train into Grand Central every day. Until we could get our apartment, we commuted together each morning. Luck or Divine Providence?

We found a nice little apartment in the neighboring community of Rye, New York, and I went to work. I had given up on suggesting that Virginia look for employment. Besides, now she was pregnant .The work was almost identical to what I had been doing in Chicago. The effort was to locate management openings wherever they might be found. This meant personally calling the human resource department of every company, big and small, and offering your service. We looked, primarily, for what we called "fee paid" openings. That meant that the company was willing to pay our fee. Most big jobs were "fee paid". Lesser jobs would be either "split fee" or client paid. Once an opening was located, we went to work to fill it using the resume's we had on file as well as all the techniques employed by "head hunters".

Each day, on my lunch break, I would go down to the street with my lunch pail. There was a bench close by where I could sit and eat and meditate. The bustle of the city would be passing by, each one on his or her little mission. I found myself looking at their faces and wondering about each one. The tourists were easy to pick out. They would be walking slowly, camera in hand, looking at everything around them. Some were shoppers carrying their new purchases. Many were office workers on lunch break. They would be walking fast, in a hurry to get where they were going. Then there would be others that you knew just by looking at them were stressed out and in trouble. Some, perhaps, were homeless; some were panhandlers. Occasionally, it would be a young girl accidentally bumping into unaccompanied men and you knew she was a "working girl". Almost without thinking, I found myself concentrating on each one and offering a silent prayer for them.

I knew what they needed and here I was trying to be New York's number one "head hunter".

This time it was me that was becoming disenchanted by my circumstance. This had been exasperated by some of the cultural shock I had experienced working for Mrs. McKay. For example, coming from my background and experience, I had always addressed those I was working with on a very personal basis by using only their given first name. One day, Mrs. McKay overheard me referring to one of my clients by his first name. After he left she called me into her office. I was expecting a word of congratulations since I had just successfully placed him on a very good job. Instead she began berating me for using his first name. In our place of business, she said, we are professionals and we will refer to our clients as Mister. If I hear you doing it again, it will be a reason for termination. Yes, New York was not like Sidney. I liked Sidney better.

My New York experience was improved temporarily by my fascination with Broadway and the Theatre. I loved music and I had read about the open auditions for Off Broadway productions. Looking at the "call sheet", a printed sheet detailing all the available auditions for the wannabee's, I saw open auditions for a musical and also a play called "Flight of the Auk" .Over the next week, I tried out for both. To my surprise, I was asked to return for a second audition for the play. The director seemed quite positive. The musical, however, gave me a part on my first audition. It was set to open much sooner than the play, so I decided to go with it and leave the play option open.

After making that decision, I was both excited and concerned heading home. Where was I going to find time for rehearsals and how was I going to fit it into my job? All I knew was, I had an itch that needed scratching. I think Virginia was more excited by it than I was. Over the next few days, we set up a game plan. Most of the rehearsals were at night. Any in the daytime we would work around one at a time. These little Off Broadway shows would come and go just as quickly. They were really opportunities for Hollywood personalities to hone their skills and newcomers to introduce themselves to a New York audience. Some would last a few weeks or months, some for only one performance. Just two weeks before opening night, I was informed that I no longer had a role. Someone from Hollywood had been given the part. I was told it was Wendell Corey. My disappointment was relieved later when this very bad musical failed to see the light of day. I turned my attention to the play. I was still in the running and the signs were positive. There was a second disappointment in store for me when the announcement came that Wendell Corey had been selected for the role I had thought might be mine. Perhaps that was all for the best. If I had gone on stage and received good reviews, I think I would have been sorely tempted to consider a career change. Was this Divine Providence at work? I guess you might say, Wendell Corey saved my bacon.

My feeling of being a "fish out of water" continued to grow, but I didn't know what to do about it. My job was going satisfactorily but I was definitely not happy. Finally, on a hunch, I called the office of the Methodist Church's New York Bishop. I don't remember who I spoke with there, but they referred me to the District Superintendent for the Kingston District. He was immediately responsive. He wanted me to come to his office as soon as possible. After sharing with him my credentials, he made a couple of calls to Nebraska. He then explained he had an opening on his district he thought was ready made for someone like me. He wanted to know when I could be available to go look. That had to be Saturday so it wouldn't interfere with work. On Saturday, he loaded Virginia and myself in his car and we headed north out of the city. It was very much like the drive up the Hudson to West Point. As we left the city behind and reached the green of the countryside, I found myself already feeling better. This was part of what I had been missing.

We drove the freeway to Kingston, then took a left on the highway to Shandaken. The District Superintendent explained that this was a four-point charge. Shandaken, Big Indian, and Pine Hill churches all had regular Sunday services. The fourth church, Oliveria, was not a regular service. I would be responsible for weddings, funerals, and other pastoral services. The parsonage was located right next door to the Shandaken church. It was a pretty two story and was looking very inviting to me. He drove us to all three towns and then back to Shandaken where an afternoon meeting had been scheduled with the leadership from the three churches with regular services. That meeting turned out to be totally positive. They agreed I could give my current employer a two week notice and then on the third week I would be in the pulpit in Shandaken. I was completely thrilled, and Virginia seemed pleased, as well.

As soon as we moved in, I threw myself into my work. My creative juices began to flow and a joy filled my heart almost beyond description. Once again, I was going to be doing the work that I was created to do, and a gracious and caring Lord had made it possible. I encouraged Virginia to read and study some of the same materials I did, and I sat a time for us to have prayer time together, just the two of us. The Sunday schedule was a grueling one. Big Indian was a nine thirty service. Shandaken was at eleven, and then Pine Hill was an evening service. When Oliveria had a service it was afternoon. One of my first orders of business was to learn where most of my people went for their medical care and to the hospital. I needed to locate a good doctor for Virginia and my Grand Island training required that I visit the hospitals on a regular basis. I learned that the closest hospital was in Margaretville and the veterans all used the Veterans Hospital in Albany, the state capitol. Those two locations became regular destinations for me. We found a good doctor for Virginia in Phoenicia which was only twenty miles from Shandaken.

There would be too much to cover if I were to try to describe all the work that was done here. I will hit some of the highlights, but they will only scratch the surface. The first thing I discovered was the people here were very provincial. Those who had been born and raised here were very suspicious of outsiders. There were a few who had moved here from the city, like our postmaster who had come from Queens, but, for the most part, they were locals, and they didn't even communicate much between the little communities I was serving. Each town was only concerned about their little piece of the world. I felt that the first thing I needed to do was find a way to create more unanimity between the churches. The answer came in the form of "The Valley Messenger". I began writing and publishing a slick finish little magazine monthly which contained local news from all three towns and with all the information about upcoming church functions with personal messages from the leadership of each church. It was the closest thing to a newspaper in the area. This was mailed to the membership and each post office had a rack for the general public. The response was electric. We saw an immediate increase in church attendance as people became more aware of what was going on, and we were able to promote some functions that could be carried out cooperatively by all of the churches. This not only got them better acquainted, but began to break down some of the barriers between them. Pine Hill, for example, was a ski resort. Their primary interest was their tourist and week-end business. That focus left little time or interest in what was happening in the rest of the valley. Big Indian and Oliveria were almost entirely composed of the families of original settlers in the area. They were the most provincial of all. They only came down from the hills when they needed supplies or medical attention, and many of them opted to care for themselves without the attention of a doctor. For some of them, not even doctors were to be trusted. I have a few copies of "The Valley Messenger" that I have saved and every now and then I look at them and am reminded of that time in New York. The paper was paid for by little advertisements from area merchants who jumped at the chance to get their message out. It was one of the most productive things I did here. There were many other things such as setting up an annual "God's Little

Acre" program. I would have a service where I would hand out $2.00 bills to every person in attendance. They were then charged to bring that back to the church on the designated day along with the increase that had come from that $2.00. The entire exercise was based on the Gospel story of "The Good and Faithful Servant". It produced amazing results. The children would get excited about little fund raising projects and the adults did everything from raising an animal to the raising of a crop from an acre of ground. Some of the women did fancy needlework to be sold at the bazaar we held at the end. The result enabled us to significantly increase our budget for missions and other charitable work by the church.

On December 17th, 1956, Virginia gave birth to my first son in the hospital in Margaretville. This seemed to me to be a life changing moment for Virginia. She now had a responsibility for something besides herself. She seemed to relish it. In my heart, I felt that maybe this was what she had needed, and just maybe, this was the Godsend that I had been hoping and praying about. We named him Anthony Lee Sample. Anthony for Virginia's stepdad and Lee after me. We designated Anthony DonGarra to be his Godfather. He was greatly honored. Mr. DonGarra had been raised in a Catholic family and the responsibility of being a Godfather was something they took quite seriously. He had become a Protestant in recent years, but the traditions of his father were still very much a part of him. We had visited his father when I was in Chicago. One weekend we went to Janesville, Wisconsin, right across the border from Illinois, and met his entire family. I really liked his dad. He was a shoe cobbler. He lived in a house where his shoe shop was right downstairs. All he had to do to go to work each day was go downstairs. He had been unable to sleep in a bed for years. He slept in his chair. He was still vibrant and very much alive. He adored his children, especially Anthony, but his other son was also a successful attorney. Not bad for an Italian immigrant that had to learn the English language after immigrating to the United States. After meeting his family, I understood the drive and ambition that Mr. DonGarra displayed. He came from strong, purpose minded, stock.

The next year was like a dream come true for me. I was completely engrossed in my work, and our location afforded me some simple pleasures that I had missed in the city. Our neighbor, directly across the street from the parsonage, was a Catholic family. She operated a hair salon out of her home and Virginia went there to get her hair done. She became good friends with the owner who would babysit our son, Tony, when needed. Her husband and I became good friends as well. He was an inveterate fly fisherman and he taught me to fly fish. It seemed he went almost every day. He was uncanny. He would see a little ripple and land his fly in just the right spot He knew exactly when to snap the line and land another nice trout. I always wondered what was his source of income. He didn't seem to have a job, but they lived very well, had a nice home with several out buildings, and I didn't think all that would be possible on what Sue was making. It would be many years before I learned the answer to that question.

Just a few years ago, I took my wife, Margaret, back to New York to visit the places I had served so many years ago. When we got to Shandaken, I took Margaret into the open church and showed her where I had preached many sermons. We walked across the street and the hair salon was still there. I knocked on the door and a gray haired lady opened it. She took one look and said in surprise, it's Rev. Sample. I said, you must be Sue Yeary. She invited us in and brought some refreshment. We sat down to visit. Mr. Yeary had passed away some years before. Sue said, "You never asked what he did for a living, but I always knew you wondered about it. It's okay to tell you now". She went to her bookshelf and took down a magazine that dealt with health foods. The lead article was about Mr. Yeary, America's king of Ginseng who passed away without revealing where his fields of Ginseng might be found. Apparently, for most of his life, he had been digging up Ginseng and selling it to buyers in New York. It was a highly profitable business for those who had access to Ginseng. According to Sue, he had found a lucrative field somewhere in the mountains. Not even Sue knew where it was located. He guarded his secret throughout his life making certain he was never followed when making his treks into the mountains. I was totally blown away. After a nice visit with Sue, we continued to the other churches. Big Indian Church had been turned into a private residence. There was a sign in front that said, "Home of the former Big Indian Methodist Church". The Pine Hill church was closed and boarded up. We could not find anyone who even remembered anyone from that time. In Oliveria, all that was left was the cemetery. We walked around and paused at the graves of those I had buried there.

Living here had reminded me of the joy of hunting and walking the great outdoors. The church and parsonage backed up to the national forest. We had a garden in back of the parsonage. At night the deer would come into the garden and eat our lettuce. It was all open field to the foot of the mountain that rose up less than a quarter mile away. Very early some mornings, I would take my twenty-two rifle and hike to the top of the first mountain and sit and meditate under a tree next to the meadow. I loved to watch the sunrise from there and listen to all the sounds of the forest. I had learned from the locals that one of their favorite dishes was made from squirrels. So, I shot a few squirrels. When Virginia refused to cook them they had to be thrown away. I didn't do that again. We did have a few bunnies and some quail. I never went after big game while in New York. We also had a very cute beagle. We had a piano in the parsonage that I enjoyed playing almost daily. I taught our little beagle to stand on the piano stool and pound the keys and howl. He was a delight to all my parishioners. One day he wandered into the street and was killed by a car. It was like losing a member of the family. We wondered how we could have been so careless as to let him get out into the street. Another lesson learned.

John Harden with his wife and new baby came to visit us one week. They had driven up from Drew University where John was attending and Joan was a teacher in town. They recounted to us their experiences of the past few years. John had married his college sweetheart who was white. They had to go to Iowa to get married because Nebraska still had a law on the books prohibiting interracial marriage. Their lives had been greatly complicated because of the prevailing public attitude on that issue. Joan was a teacher, and she feared to include John in school functions lest it become cause for her dismissal. By the same token, John's counselors at Drew were telling him that it was going to be next to impossible for him to find employment in the church. He would likely not be welcomed in a black church. A white church was just as problematic. I will jump ahead in the story to tell you that John ultimately became a Chaplain for the state of New York. They serviced all the prisons in the state. Within a few years he became head of the department. Unfortunately, in the 70's he was killed in a tragic automobile accident and Joan went home to Apple Valley, California, with her three children. I have had no further contact, but I pray they are doing well. After a good visit with John and Joan, they went home without staying for the Sunday church service. They were afraid it might create controversy for me.

Another tragic event occurred while we were there. Beth and Chuck's daughter had just turned sixteen and she had her first driver's license. Virginia, and her little cousin, had done some bonding while we were in White Plains. She decided to come up and visit. I was surprised that Chuck gave her permission; but, both Beth and Chuck were pushovers for their daughter. Coming through Phoenicia, a young boy on a bicycle drove out directly in front of her car. She swerved, trying to avoid him, but instead it was a direct hit and he was killed instantly. I received a call from the police and drove immediately into Phoenicia. At the police station they told me she was not to blame. She had done everything possible to avoid him, even going into the ditch. There would be no charges, but she was badly shaken and the car was in the shop for minor repairs. I took her home and she stayed with us for the next few days. Somewhat to my surprise, Chuck and Beth did not come up. When the car was repaired she drove it home.

The truth is, I would have been perfectly happy to remain in this idyllic community for the rest of my natural life. I was good for them, and they were good for me. Tony was not six months old before Virginia was again showing signs of being restless and unhappy. I had always thought, having met her in church, she shared my Christian values. That was something I was beginning to question. She seemed to resent what I was doing and would go out of her way to embarrass me. For example, one day she walked to the liquor store and bought a quart of beer. Then, without putting it in a bag, she marched through town and into the post office to get the mail before going home. It was no big deal, except it was quite obvious it was done to embarrass me. I did not drink beer and she hadn't shown any interest in it before. Little things like that kept happening. She would fail to show up for one of the ladies meetings where she was expected. She was showing, in any way she could, she did not enjoy being a pastors wife. This was despite the fact the church people had been ebullient in their acceptance of her. They fawned over Tony from the day he was born. Things continued like this until one day I came home and Virginia was gone. She had taken Tony and gone back to the city to Beth and Chuck's house. A call confirmed that she was there. At church I covered for her saying she had gone to visit her relatives. Another call a few days later confirmed what I had been expecting. Virginia said she had no intention of returning unless I would agree to get her out of Shandaken. Unless I was willing to get into another line of work, she was done. This was a familiar story; but, I knew she really had no place to go and no tools for coping with the responsibility of raising and providing for a child. Beth and Chuck would not have put up with her for long and then what? What would become of Tony? I called the District Superintendent and told him I needed to speak with him on an urgent basis. He came to see me the next day. After explaining everything to him we had a prayer together and talked some more. He said he understood why I wanted to try to hold my family together and even though he would hate to see me leave he thought it might be easier than trying to stay. Two weeks later, after excuses to my flock and a heart rending send-off dinner, we were on our way to Denver with a stop -over in Chicago.

When we arrived in Denver, we stayed with my parents for the first week. My father was having a hard time trying to understand what was happening. I had not shared with my family any of the trauma I had experienced over the past couple of years. It was my thought it was best to keep that to myself; but, I could tell my dad suspected. It showed in his attitude. I now had to find new employment. This time it took longer. Good jobs were not that plentiful and my liberal arts degree wasn't doing me much good. Finally, I got an offer from International Harvester as a traveling sales rep. It would pay $400.00 a month plus expenses. They would be ready for me to start in one month. In the meantime, I needed to earn some money another way. I answered an ad in the paper for a sales rep. for the Grolier Society. It was a door to door job selling encyclopedias. After the interview, the District Sales Manager, Bill Stephan, convinced me to go with him on some presentations and see what it was like. Thinking I had nothing to lose, I agreed. The presentation was impressive and the offer looked to me like one I would buy. They were offering a complete twenty volume set of the Book of Knowledge, a ten volume set of science books, seven volumes of Lands and Peoples, a two volume set of Webster's Dictionaries, a twenty volume set of Grolier Encyclopedias, and a bookcase all for just $399.00. This could be paid with $10, 00 down and the balance at $10.00 a month. After watching a few presentations with Bill, I took a sales kit and went on my own. The hard part was getting invited into a home to make a presentation; but, when I was able to do that, my close rate was over 50%. In the first week I made more in commissions than the job I was waiting for would pay in a month. My success was based mainly in the fact that I felt I was doing the family a real service. I was putting in their children's hands the tools for a good education. I knew it was a product I would use, and it was important that those tools be conveniently available to their children. I called International Harvester and told them I had accepted another job. Working directly under Bill Stephan, I was soon promoted to Manager of the Denver District. Virginia and I moved into a very nice house on the west side of Denver that had a large family room that I could use for recruiting sales people. We were, also, able to use it as a phone operation to set up appointments for the salesmen. Everything seemed to be going well. Even Virginia seemed to be happier. She enjoyed talking with the sales reps and getting coffee for them. Also, she was pregnant again. This, too, seemed to make her happy. Our second son, Andrew Johnson Sample, was born on April 8th of 1958. Johnson had been Mrs. DonGarra's first husband's name. He was Virginia's real father. He had been a professional golfer, but I never knew any of the details of that history.

As sales in Denver become harder, I began taking crews and going on the road to smaller communities around the state. We found they were more receptive to what we had to offer. Many did not have good libraries for their children and having it right at home was a blessing. Then something happened that totally surprised my father. My brother, Robert, had suffered a double hernia operation from his work as a body and fender man and he was out of work. He needed to find something he could do that was not so strenuous. I said, Bob, why don't you come and ride with me for a week and see what I do? Maybe, you could do it too. I will pay your expenses, so you won't be out anything. Dad heard what he was planning and took me aside. He said, you know Robert doesn't speak very well. You are leading him into a pit. I said, Dad, after this week Robert will know for himself if that is true. In the meantime there is no harm done. He's not working and I will enjoy his company for a week.

We headed up to Glenwood Springs and checked into a motel. In the next three days, Robert watched me make presentations to about ten or twelve different families resulting in six sales. He asked me how much that meant to me in commissions. When I told him he couldn't believe it. He said, that doesn't really seem that hard at all. I think I could do that. It was our method of operation to use days to set appointments for the evening when both parents would be home. We were sometimes able to do that during the day, but that was the exception. We used all kinds of means to find out who had children in school so we didn't waste time on people who were not prospects. To make a long story short, on the first ever presentation by Robert, he came out with a sale. I had waited for him in the car. He was soaked in sweat and a little bit giddy, but he had been successful. From the start, he was a bulldog. What he lacked in finesse he made up for in determination. When we got back to Denver, Robert was a new man. His confidence matched his new sense of worth, and Dad had to admit that maybe he had been wrong. Over the next year, Robert set sales records in the Denver office and became a manager himself taking crews on the road.

A few months later, I was offered the job as Manager for the state of Montana and the northern half of Wyoming. It would mean moving to Billings, but the increased income would mean we could buy a house. In late 1958 we moved to Billings. The home we purchased was walking distance to shopping and other services, and it was also close to the Methodist Church. The pastor was someone I knew from the past at Wesleyan. It was like old home week. Again I began to feel at home. Montana was beautiful and the sales were going well. Again, Virginia was pregnant. It seemed to be the only thing that made her happy. Things were on a steady keel for the next few months. On November 20th of 1959 our daughter, Alexis Dianne Sample, was born. Virginia's little sister, Judy, who had just graduated high school came out on an extended visit. Her reason was to help out Virginia with the baby, but I think her main reason was to get away from people in Evanston that had been giving her trouble. I think her parents with all they had on their plate were rather neglectful of their daughter. Plus, we had just learned that Anthony was suffering some serious problems with his diabetes. He had suffered with diabetes for years but had been able to control it with insulin shots. It was a dark cloud that hung over their head.

Judy seemed to enjoy living with us. It gave Virginia someone to talk to and Judy began to confide in me the issues that were bothering her from Chicago. I won't talk about all she told me, but she responded positively to my counseling. She also confided in me to tell me of some the issues she had with her sister, Virginia, and her behavior. She was fearful that it might happen again. I think she may have been trying to give me a warning of things that maybe she knew that I didn't. But, I didn't pick up on that at the time. Virginia convinced me that she needed an automobile to give her more mobility for shopping and doctors visits with the children which made perfect sense. I got her an automobile. She and Judy were free to tool around Billings.

A few weeks later while on a road trip to Great Falls with my crew, I got a strange call in the middle of the week. Barry Bulgart was at my home in Billings and needed to see me. Barry was definitely not one of my favorite people. He had worked for me in Denver as one of my salesmen, but he had done me wrong. In Colorado, I had developed a little hobby of taking a sensitive Geiger counter and walking into the mountains to prospect for uranium. Uranium was a big topic in the late 50's and early 60's. I didn't really expect to find anything, but it gave me an excuse to hike in the mountains and who knows, maybe, get lucky. One day Barry Bulgart asked if he could borrow my Geiger counter. He and some friends were going to go to the mountains that week-end, and they thought it would be fun to do what I had been doing. I said fine. Just be careful with it. It had been rather expensive. The following week he did not bring it back. When asked about it, he said he had it at home, but he would bring it by as soon as he could. Instead he disappeared not to be seen again. A long time later, I learned from one of the other salesmen, Barry had hocked my Geiger counter. A tour of the pawn shops revealed that it had already been taken out of hock and sold by the shop. All that was left was a bitter taste in my mouth, and now here he was at my home in Billings. I gave one of my salesmen the responsibility of helping the rest of the crew and I went home early.

It was late evening when I got home. To my surprise, Virginia had on her best nightgown she only wore for me on special occasions. I wondered about it, but didn't say anything. Barry and two of his friends were sleeping outside in a camper. I decided to wait till morning to confront him. When I did, my first comment was that I knew he had hocked my Geiger counter and lost it. I said, you owe me for it. He then launched into a long story about being in financial trouble in Denver and needing money to get back home. He didn't think he had another choice. He would be glad to pay me back and he had brought two good men with him and they would all three like to work for me in Montana. I learned that they had all been there for two days already and Virginia had been treating them like royalty, feeding them and giving them the run of the house. Nothing about this smelled right to me. I told Barry, I have nothing for you in Montana. If you want to go back to Denver and talk to them, be my guest, but I have nothing for you or your friends. I will expect you to pay back your debt to me and if that does not happen, I may press charges. I want you out of my home forthwith. I never heard from Barry Bulgart again and, of course, never got any of my money back.

It was only a short time later, I received another call while on the road. It was from my next door neighbor. She had been calling everywhere to find out where I was, but when she found me she said, "I think you had better get home. I saw Virginia load up the car with all her belongings and the children and they have been gone since yesterday." It had happened again. I rushed back to Billings to an empty house. A quick check revealed that the bank account was totally drained and was in fact over-drawn. A check of my credit card revealed that it had been maxed out. Later I would learn that I owed a local shop for a set of new tires and some other mechanical work. She was somewhere on the road with my children. I felt a deep sense of despair. My first thought was my friend at the Methodist Church. For the first time, I gave him the complete history of our marriage. He said, Rex, you have no choice but to get yourself the best lawyer you can and we have one right here in the church. One call and I was in to see the attorney. After recounting to him all that I had shared with my pastor, he said, Rex, there is only one thing I need to know. Do you want your children? They will be a big responsibility, but I need to know if you want them? My response was immediate. Of course, I want my children. Then, he said, you need to do exactly what I tell you to do. There will be times when you will not like me for it. In fact, you may end up hating me, but it is the only way for you. I agreed and he explained. He said, in the past when Virginia has left and then run into trouble, she has always had a place to retreat. You have been that enabler that has given her back safe haven. This time that needs to be different. There should be nothing here for her. I want you to sell the house and all the furniture. You go on the road and leave all the rest to me.

The house was an easy sell and my next door neighbor helped me dispose of the furniture. Before that was complete, I received an unexpected call from a repair shop in Miles City, Montana. He said, he had a car there that hadn't been picked up and his bill needed to be paid or he would sell the car. He found my number on a receipt in the glove box. I took one of my salesmen and drove to Miles City to retrieve the car. It still had most of the things she had taken from the house and a lot of her clothes. Apparently, the car had broken down outside of Miles City and it had been towed to the shop. Some local checking with the Miles City police revealed that they had spent one night at the hotel and then had taken the train on to Chicago. I had already spoken with the DonGarra's but they had not heard from Virginia. Neither they, nor I, had any idea where she might be with the children. After paying the shop with some of the money from the sale of the house, I took the car back to Billings. It was apparent to me that Virginia was going to be in trouble soon. It must have taken a good part of her money to get to Chicago, and, who knows what her circumstances are there. Following the instructions from my attorney, I tried to put that out of my mind and go on the road and work.

Within three weeks, I received a call from my attorney. Virginia was back in Billings. I would learn later that she had used up the rest of her money hotel hopping in Chicago with the children. Apparently, she had someone there, I presume a man, had conspired with her for her return to Chicago. He must have thought better of it and left her high and dry. She had not only used all her money but had written bad checks to the hotel. I had closed my account in Billings and opened a new one, so the checks she had written bounced and she had been arrested by the police. When she became desperate she called her parents. They covered her checks and got her released from police custody. They told her she was not welcome with them. Go home with the children and we will pay for your ticket.

When I got to Billings, I went directly to my lawyer's office. There I learned it was feta compli. When Virginia had arrived home and found the house was gone, she had taken the children to the pastor's house. There she learned I had filed for divorce and they gave her the lawyers name and information. She left the children with the pastor and his wife and went to my lawyer's office. There she signed the "no contest" divorce papers granting me full custody of the children in return for $500.00, which my lawyer paid to her, and a ticket back to Chicago. She was already gone. My attorney had said I might end up hating him. He was close to right. I was angry I had not had opportunity to confront her. My lawyer said, if I had given you that opportunity you may very well of started this whole charade all over again. I was acting in your best interest. It would be some time before I could accept that. But, my life would now be set on a different course.

What are we to conclude from all of this? Certainly, we can suggest that we should all "look before we leap". You could be deaf, blind, and dumb and still see that my first marriage was a mistake. Youth, naiveté, and a lack of willingness to listen to counsel, had made it possible. But, after we have made that mistake, what then? Are we to regret the birth of three divinely created human beings? One's that we love? Does that mistake forever brand us in a way that is irretrievable? I will have much more to say about that in my final chapter. The one thing I can say here is in my own mind and heart I believed I could never again enter the pulpit. A pastor is supposed to lead by example. I had violated all my vows. The ministry was no place for a divorced man, and certainly not a hypocrite.

7

Learning to Swim

NOW, I HAD A MORE IMMEDIATE PROBLEM. WHAT DO I do with the children? They were at the pastor's house. Tony was only four, Andrew was still being potty trained, and Alexis was a baby in diapers. There was a woman in our church that had helped Virginia with the children from time to time. She was a Swedish lady with two children of her own. She agreed to take the children temporarily until I could figure out my next move. That next move proved to be resigning my manager's job in Montana and moving back to Denver with Mother and Dad and Dorothy. Dorothy had no children of her own and she relished the opportunity to be Mother to mine, if only, temporarily. That time with the children resulted in a bonding between Alexis and Dorothy that lasted for the remainder of Dorothy's life. As Alexis grew to be an adult, she and Dorothy shared with each other and helped each other like mother and daughter. Their secrets remain their own.

I had resigned my manager's job, but I hadn't left Grolier. They chose to select me to be a National Trainer headquartered out of Denver. This would entail covering thirteen states training sales reps. The job carried a nice salary plus commission on any personal sales. With my children safe, and with the pain of my divorce beginning to fade, I threw myself back into my work. The Regional Manager for Grolier, Jack Hemphill, insisted that his National Trainer had to put on an impressive front when training new reps. This included leasing a new Lincoln Continental. I was covering my thirteen states behind the wheel of my Lincoln. I must say, it was a great car but, I always felt a bit of a hypocrite. The one thing that was different in this new job was it meant I would be in the local office every week and sometimes every day. This resulted in an event that would change my life forever.

The young lady that took the orders from the sales reps and processed them, was an attractive lady with a warm smile and a personality that charmed all the reps. Her name was Margaret. I had noticed that most of the reps would hit on her. She had a way of swatting them away like flies, but without offending. That, in itself, is a real talent. It became very obvious to me she had absolutely no interest in getting mixed up with a salesman. Over the next few months, I found myself seeking out little excuses to visit with Margaret. Maybe checking on an order, or getting supplies, or whatever would occur to me. I instinctively knew she was someone I wanted to know better. Finally, one day I got up the courage to say to her, Margaret, would you like to meet me for coffee after work. I would like to get to know you better. To my surprise, she said yes. Later, over coffee, I learned she had been born and raised on a farm in South Dakota. Her background and mine were very similar. In fact, we discovered we had a whole lot in common. She had been confirmed in the Lutheran Church, but our values were very much in sync. The big difference was she had never been married whereas I had three children. I shared with her all that history, but instead of running for the door, she agreed to a dinner date the next week. I took her to a fancy French Restaurant and the waiter talked us into trying their frogs' legs. I'm sure neither of us enjoyed those stringy morsels, but we didn't complain. At least the dessert was good. Shortly thereafter, Margaret invited me to come to her house for dinner. She lived with her best friend, Mary Urkalek. She served me a spaghetti dinner. It was great.

After those first few dates, Margaret became my only feminine interest. I sensed from the beginning that she was the "one ". I wondered how she would feel about the children. Some of that concern was assuaged after the first time I took her to meet my parents and the children. Tony and Drew both went to her like they had known her forever. Dad took me aside and said, son, this one is a keeper, don't let her get away. He had always been rather cool around Virginia. I realized then that my father's instincts were better than my own. Over the next few months, Margaret and I made a point of doing things with the children, visits to the zoo, going to the park or on a picnic, anything we could do together. The children were beginning to bond with Margaret, and she with them. I think her brothers were mortified. Margaret came from a close knit family and had an older brother and two younger brothers. They were very protective of their little sister and seeing her begin to get serious about a salesman with three children must have been difficult for them. Yet, they were never anything but respectful to me.

My first proposal of marriage was met with a, I have to think about it response. I'm certain that answer was entirely appropriate. After all, taking on the responsibility of being Mother to three young children was a monumental undertaking. After having time to consider, she said, yes. The wedding was held at University Park United Methodist Church on September 8th, 1962. It was a grand wedding. Margaret's sisters were bridesmaids and her younger brothers were ushers. George, her elder brother, led her down the aisle to be given away. While standing at the altar and watching the processional coming toward me, I remember thinking, this has all been made possible by a gracious and caring God. He has blessed me with his favor. But the most touching moment was still to come. My family was all there and Mother and Dorothy were taking care of the children in the third or fourth pew. As Margaret and George reached the pew where the children were, my son, Drew, who was not yet quite four years old, stood up on the pew and yelled out so that everyone in church could hear it, "that's my mommy". Indeed, she was.

Since both Margaret and I worked for Grolier and my manager, Ed Riggs, had been my best man, Grolier decided to pay for our honeymoon. That included a trip to Las Vegas. However, it did carry one caveat. The New Mexico State Fair was about to begin and Grolier had booked a large booth in the display area. We were to come back from Las Vegas by way of Albuquerque and manage the booth for the fair along with three of our best salesmen. This we gladly did. They had booked us into a very nice motel and it was just an extension of our honeymoon. One thing did occur, however, that would have a bearing on events in years to come. On lunch breaks I would wander around the fair and take in the sights. One day that included stopping by the track where the horses were running. I carried a pass that was good for about everything at the fair including going into the grandstand. The horses were just coming onto the track for the next race. I knew a little about horses and looking at the odds board I was confused. The four horse, who was an almost even money favorite was washing badly. That can be caused just because it's a warm day and the horse is hot; but most of the time it indicates extreme nervousness and tension. It is never a good sign. On the other hand, the nine horse, who was 18/1 on the odds board looked magnificent to me. His ears were perked, he was calm, and on his toes. I walked to the betting window and bought a $2.00 ticket on the nine to win. When he crossed the line first, I collected my $38.00 and went back to the booth. Later, I would share my little success story with Margaret along with a little braggadocio. The seed had been sown for what could become a problem later on.

That little seed became larger with another event that occurred soon after. Grolier had a very good re-load salesman that covered all thirteen states in our region. A re-load salesman was one who would call on previous customers who had the Grolier library with a courtesy call and then would attempt to sell them on additional items such as the Americana Encyclopedia. This man had been extremely successful at his job but, he had run into a snag. He had purchased a racing quarter horse named Dirty Leo. He was the grandson of a famous sire called Leo. Following his horse from track to track and paying for his trainer and his up-keep had caused his sales production to drop off to practically nothing and he was approaching bankruptcy. Ed Riggs, his manager, had a place in the suburbs of Denver that had a horse barn and his son was wanting a horse to ride. Ed Riggs agreed to bail him out and purchase Dirty Leo. Our re-load man was able to go back to work and become productive again but, it didn't work so well for Ed Riggs. Dirty Leo was too much for his son to handle. He was not a riding horse, he was a racehorse.

I had an idea. Margaret's sister, Doris, was married to a man who owned a gas station in Boulder. Not only that, he raised and raced horses, both quarters and thoroughbreds. I called Cliff and said, do you have a good riding horse that you might be willing to trade for a racing quarter horse out of Leo. His response was a resounding yes. I then went to Ed Riggs and said, my wife's brother-in-law has a nice gently riding horse he would be willing to trade you for Dirty Leo. Cliff brought his horse down to Denver in the horse trailer and Ed's son had a chance to ride her. It was love at first sight. The trade was made, everybody was happy. Cliff put Dirty Leo on the track in Denver at Centennial Race Track. Whenever he would run, if I was in town, I would go to watch him run. When Cliff retired him, he was able to sell him to a horse rancher in Nebraska that planned to use him as stud. Cliff had also been successful with the thoroughbreds he had raised. One of his three year olds won the Colorado Breeders Cup, and Cliff was honored as horseman of the year. In the process of all this, I was becoming quite proficient at handicapping a race. It would have been much better had I been lousy at it but, I was actually quite good. My success had caused me to enjoy it too much. It was not a problem now, but was destined to become a problem in the future.

In 1960 I lost my father. A fatal stroke took his life. I look back on that week with much regret. I had been scheduled for a trip to Kansas, but before I left Dad and I had a disagreement. I don't even remember what it was about. All I remember is that some harsh words were spoken. It was while I was gone that his stroke occurred. My final words with him had been unpleasant ones. That has been a source of regret for many years. Let it be a lesson to my readers. Make a conscious effort with those you love to never leave them with animus. No one knows the day or the hour.

The first couple of years were difficult ones for Margaret. When we got back from our honeymoon, I had to go back on the road. She was left with the children and on that very first trip both Tony and Drew came down with Chicken Pox. As sick as they were, Margaret, being Margaret, was able to deal with it but, this and some subsequent illnesses with the children made us both realize that I needed to be home more. I had a good job, but being gone five days a week was an inordinate burden on Margaret. I began looking to see if I could find another employment option that would get me off the road. This search resulted in my being hired by Prentice Hall. I left Grolier on good terms and many of the good friends I developed there remained my good friends till this very day. The job at Prentice Hall was selling law books to law libraries and law firms and tax libraries to accounting firms. My territory was Denver, Colorado Springs and surrounding areas. The job carried a nice salary plus bonuses and health insurance. All went well and being home every night was a blessing. Especially, being able to sit down to a home cooked meal each night. It was considerably different than what I had experienced in the five years before when I had found myself doing much of the cooking.

In my second year, Prentice Hall sent me to their national convention in San Francisco along with the Rep. for the rest of Colorado. He and I had become good friends. Ken was in the habit of playing practical jokes on people and that little idiosyncrasy was about to show itself again. At the convention, the two of us went to dinner at a nice hotel with an orchestra and a dance floor. My buddy left the table, I presumed to go to the bathroom. Instead, I found the spotlight from the stage was shining on me and I heard the bandleader say, I have just been informed that we have in our audience tonight a young man fresh from the Chicago club circuit. Let's all get our hands together and see if we can encourage Rex Sample to come up and do a number with the orchestra. Red from ear to ear, not really knowing what to do, I went to the stage. I asked the band leader if they had an arrangement of "I Left My Heart in San Francisco". He said, are you kidding, that's our staple. So we did it. It actually went well and no one knew it had been only a practical joke. Later I told my buddy, Ken, I was going to choke him, but he thought it was funny and the best joke he'd been able to carry out. I often wondered if anybody tried to figure out who this Rex Sample was from the Chicago club circuit.

It was at this time we moved from our home in north Denver to a place called the Bell Ranch. It was a nice size ranch on the northeast side of Denver. We had been wanting a place that had room for a garden and a place we could have chickens and some geese. We rented the buildings, but Mr. Bell still drove out from town and took care of the ranch. The ranch had two houses on it. The family that had the other one rented turned out to be a rather strange bunch as my children discovered. They had three children, two boys and a girl. As would be quite normal they ended up riding the school bus together and playing together. After school one day, the oldest boy took his air rifle and went out to play with A.J. A.J. is what Andrew had come to be called. Some called him Drew, but A.J. is what stuck. Sometime later Margaret saw him return to the yard without A.J. She went out and asked where A.J. was. He said, oh he is laying out there in the field pretending to be hurt. He's okay. Margaret asked him what happened and he said, oh we were playing and I pretended to shoot him, but my rifle was empty, so

I know he's all right. She asked just where he was. I was at work. Margaret made a quick walk to the field and found him on the ground and definitely hurt. The ambulance was called and A.J. transported to the emergency room. By this time, a furious father had been informed and headed to the hospital. X-rays revealed a pellet lodged very close to the heart. The surgeon explained that his only option was to do surgery and he scheduled in for the next day. I returned to the farm and went immediately to the neighbor's house to speak with the father and his son. A.J. had told me that they were playing and he had put the rifle right against his back and pulled the trigger. At first the father was totally defensive and angry that I would be accusing his son of anything. When he learned A.J. was facing what amounted to open heart surgery, his attitude changed and he began to berate his boy and even cuff him around. Through it all the boy insisted he did not think his rifle was loaded. I asked him why, when A.J. insisted he was hurt, did you just leave him lying there and not seek help. Again he said, because I thought he was faking it. With nothing more to be accomplished here, I went home wondering what I was going to do next. I knew it had to be reported, but I wasn't sure what I would say. The next afternoon we went to the hospital for the surgery. They were just taking A.J. in for prep. About one half hour later the surgery nurse came out and said, there has been a delay. We did one more X-ray to identify the exact location of the pellet and when we did, we couldn't find the pellet. We are doing additional X-rays now to find it. We will get back to you as soon as we have more information. It was nearly an hour before the surgeon came out to see us. He was smiling from ear to ear. He said, I have a rather remarkable story to tell you, but it's all good. Our X-rays had shown the pellet to be lodged next to the heart; but, in fact, it had penetrated the wall of the esophagus. Overnight it had made its journey through the body and they found it in the bowel. He said, it will be another thirty minutes or so, but A.J. can go home with you. When we got home the authorities had been there to question the neighbor boy. After speaking with them, they asked if I wanted to press charges. At this point, a very relieved and grateful parent, knowing that we had, indeed, dodged a bullet, decided it was best to let the issue drop.

The Bell ranch brought us a number of other little adventures. It was here that A.J. hurt himself sledding down the hill in the snow. He hit a barbed wire fence and slashed his neck till it looked like someone had tried to decapitate him. That one took a long time to heal. He carries the scar yet today. It was here that Alexis had her regular run-in with our main rooster. The rooster had learned that Alexis was afraid of him. Every day when the school bus would get home, that rooster would wait for Alexis to get off the bus. When she did, he would wait for her to get about 200 feet from the house. Then he would charge her. Alexis would shriek in fright and the rooster would chase her all the way to the door. The rooster would then flap his wings and let out a mighty crow. It was his entertainment for the day. This went on for some time till one day I came home to find the rooster was in Margaret's stew pot .She had the last word.

A.J. was now twelve years old and beginning to do some things that would remind me of myself at that age. He had been going down to the neighbors' farm, about one half mile away, and buying raw milk for Margaret. Both Margaret and I had been raised on raw milk, and we preferred it for the children. While there, he had become acquainted with the farmer. The farmer told A.J. he could use a little help around the farm if he was inereste4d. A.J. jumped at the chance. He began working with the cattle and doing other chores around the place. When he came home with his first paycheck, he was one proud boy, and we were proud of him.

We remained here until Mr. Bell became disabled and decided to sell the ranch. We then moved our entire menagerie to a similar place in Franktown south of Denver. It, also, had a place to buy raw milk at a small dairy right next door as well as a place for our chickens and a nice garden plot. Now, both of the boys were wanting to find a way to make some money. We answered an ad in the Rocky Mountain News and Tony and A.J. ended up with a contract to deliver all the papers for the Rocky Mountain News in Franktown and Castle Rock, including all the paper dispensers abound town. This meant that Margaret and I had to take turns getting up at 4:30 and taking one of the boys on the route. We would be done before time to catch the school bus. It was a hassle, but it was good for the boys and they enjoyed it. They had to share a portion of their new found income to cover the cost of gas, but they did so gladly and were proud of themselves.

It was here in Franktown that Judy, Nan's younger daughter came to live with us. She had been living in Breckenridge with her husband and working for one of the ski lodges; but, one day he just abandoned her and went to California. Judy was quite broken up and came to live with us for a time. She had a horse that was her pride and joy and one that was fully spoiled. Jester, I don't think, had any great credentials, but Judy loved him and my children were thrilled to have him around as well. After a time, she decided to move to California. Her sister Virginia, had birthed two more children before being divorced by her second husband. She had met someone else and had remarried for the third time and was living in California with him and her two children. I never knew what the conversations were between Judy and Virginia, but she decided to take Jester and move to California. It was, no doubt, best all around.

8

Becoming an Entrepreneur

MY JOB WITH PRENTICE HALL TOOK ME INTO EVERY major law firm and accounting firm in the entire Denver and Colorado Springs area and this led to a new opportunity. One day I received a call from a man I had never met who said that it was imperative that I speak with him. He had something very important to discuss. I agreed to meet him for coffee at a local motel restaurant. It turned out to be Jack Cleary, a very charming and debonair gentleman of about forty years of age. He explained that he had been trying to reach me for some time, but it took a while to track me down. He had just launched a new project called American Tax Aids. This was to be a series of franchised tax offices that he envisioned would cover the entire country and be a rival to H&R Block. He had recruited the former head of the IRS to be President of the company and it was their desire to have highly trained agents that would have a technical back-up system so they could offer a far more professional service than the other national companies were providing at that time. Plus, his IRS connection, they believed, would give them national credibility. Their financing was all in place, all the legal work had been done, their office was open, and they were ready to launch. They had been looking for someone to come in as Vice-President in charge of sales. They wanted someone who was familiar with the subject and someone who would have an entree into the possible prospects in the Colorado market. That search had turned up my name. I met the President and sensed his enthusiasm for the project. He told me he had excellent contacts all around the country, but wanted to get the local and area markets up and running in the first year before launching out nationally. They had planned for an aggressive television and radio advertising package to support any new franchise locations and the neon signs that had been designed for each office location were very impressive. Needless to say, I was flattered and also impressed. After discussing it with Margaret, I agreed. Now, I guess, I am an entrepreneur, or trying to become one.

This turned out to be the hardest job I had done up to that point in my life. We were really starting from scratch. We needed to develop a sales presentation, presentation materials both printed and video, prospect lists, and then do the work to make the contacts and sell the franchises. We decided, early on, that we would only sell individual offices in the greater Denver area and our head office would be the area franchise holder. In other areas of the country, we would sell an entire area so one owner who could have multiple sub-franchises under him. This could allow the company to grow expeditiously. In the first few months I was able to sell out the Denver area. This was followed by Longmont and Fort Collins. We knew we were under the gun to get offices open and running in time for the new tax season in January. The decision was made, primarily at the wishes of our President, to go ahead and launch offices right in the home territory of H&R Block in Kansas City. I was not altogether in favor of that move, but I agreed to it.

A few phone calls and some tricks I had learned in the headhunting business turned up some good prospects. Jack Cleary and I prepared to go to Kansas City. Jack was a pilot and had a Cessna single engine prop. We flew to Kansas City and within a week we had successfully sold the area franchise to a local accounting office that was anxious to expand. We called our President, and he was thrilled. I think he was wanting to send a message to H&R Block. I still believe that there had been bad blood between that firm and the IRS when he was commissioner; but that suspicion was never confirmed. On the way home from Kansas City, I had one of the scariest moments of my young life. Our flight was uneventful until we reached western Kansas. At that point, Jack picked up information on a major storm that was kicking up in eastern Colorado. He could not see a way around it. Our final Omni station was in Goodland, Kansas. Jack called them and they said the weather was clear in Denver, so Jack decided to try to gain enough altitude to get on top of the storm and then it would be clear to land in Denver. That plan didn't work. The storm was a lot bigger and more severe than he had concluded. As we crossed into Colorado the storm had become so intense that all you could see in the windshield of the plane was the snow and ice pelting against the window. In a matter of minutes, the wings of the plane began to ice and it was becoming harder to hold. I could see that Jack was very concerned. He said, I need to reach someone on the radio and see if there is some place we can set her down. He said, Rex, I want you to take the controls for just a few minutes until I can reach somebody. The plane had a horizon finder right on the instrument panel. He said, don't look at the windshield. Just look at the horizon finder and keep it steady and level to the horizon and keep the nose up, I will do the rest. So, my first flying lesson was going to be in a snow storm. Jack was frantically trying to reach anyone, but the radio just crackled and popped. My few minutes turned into what seemed an eternity with my eyes glued to the horizon finder. Then, as if by magic, we flew into a clear sky and could see in the distance the lights of Denver. Jack took back the controls and called for landing instructions from the Denver airport. My silent prayer had been answered. I remembered all those others that had been lost in small plane crashes because of underestimating storms. Buddy Holly and

Audie Murphy's deaths had not been that long ago. We were very fortunate or maybe we had an Angel for a co-pilot. Not me, I'm no Angel, but my fellow believers will know what I mean.

As tax season approached, the company launched the advertising campaign. The commercials featured the expertise of our agents and promised to represent any audited clients with the IRS. It appeared that the response had been favorable. Each office was offering year around service to businesses as well as bookkeeping services. It was my belief that for our first year we had met most of our goals. It had not really been a whole year. It was part of a year and one tax season. I was soon to have a rude awakening. Our President was an excellent tax man and was extremely knowledgeable about the tax code, but he was a lousy business man and a poor manager. Forty years later, I can believe that about an ex IRS commissioner. The cat was out of the bag when the company couldn't come up with my salary. They had put all of their money into the ad campaign without any contingency planning. I had never been a part of the financial side of the business. I was always told that the company was well financed. After just one year, American Tax Aids folded. The individual offices survived, but most of them changed their name.

As the saga with American Tax Aids was playing out, a tragedy occurred with the DonGarra's. I told you earlier that Anthony had been battling diabetes since his early twenties. It was now going to take his life. It began with just a sore on his foot that would not heal. It ended up killing him. "Little Stars" had already been canceled by WGN. Virginia's program had been cancelled as well. My ex-wife, Virginia, had remarried and had started a new family. She had managed to alienate herself from her parents. Throughout the process of my divorce, I had been able to maintain a good relationship with both of the DonGarra's. They had done all they could think of to do over the five years of our marriage to be helpful and they were both attached to their grandchildren. Now, with Anthony gone as well as the income from all of his enterprises,

Virginia was faced with the prospect of staying in Chicago and starting over or to come to Denver where she could be close to her grandchildren and do something there. Margaret graciously extended the invitation to her to come and live with us until she found what she wanted to do. That was the option she chose.

I believe it was sometimes difficult for Margaret to have the Mother of my ex-wife living with us, but since Virginia had never made any attempt to contact or see her children and was now remarried, she accepted and dealt with it. The children all called Mrs. DonGarra, Nan, Italian for grandmother. She arrived at a transition time. American Tax Aids had folded and I had been scratching around for my next project. I had been given a taste of becoming an entrepreneur and I liked the feel of it. I had been going to a barbershop in north Denver that gave razor cuts. Fiore's was the only shop in town that did that. I thought, why not franchise barbershops that do razor cuts. I talked to Mr. Fiore about it and he liked the idea. I put a complete franchise proposal together, but it didn't take root. Then, I thought, why not set up an ad agency. I began by gathering all the materials for building brochures for motels and hotels, and advertising postcards that motels and hotels could use for their promotion. Guests could use the postcards to send a message home and it would feature a picture of the motel or hotel. I found a reasonable receptive market. As that little idea began to take root, I expanded its scope by going to dude ranches around the state and selling them on brochures, and to RV parks and other types of businesses. One project came as the result of a chance phone call. I went to Dallas and did the brochure for the School of Fine Arts. It was also a modeling agency.

It was at this point that Nan entered the picture. She was no stranger to advertising, so we teamed up to try to get a foothold in the Denver market. So, where do you go to find clients that might need your service? Answer, shopping centers. Most large shopping centers have an on-site promotion or advertising office. A little research revealed that the Alameda Shopping Center did not have one. Yet, their center had two major retailers. A little salesmanship convinced their management that it was a good idea. We were given office space and became the exclusive agency for the center. Each month we published a newspaper size flyer that was distributed by hand to every home in that area of Denver featuring the specials from every shop in the center as well as full page ads from the majors. We were not exactly cutting a fat hog, but we were making a living and thinking of other projects.

One day, out of the blue, an old acquaintance of mine from Grolier came into my office. He had worked in a different territory than me covering Nevada and part of California, but we had met. He said, I heard that you are in the advertising business now and I have a little job for you. He went on to explain that he was no longer with Grolier, but had branched out on his own and currently had several projects he was working on. He had met a couple of guys in Las Vegas that needed some help with some new products they had developed, but he didn't have time to do what needed to be done. He told them he was going to Denver, and he knew someone there that he thought could help them. That someone was me. I asked him what kind of products we were talking about. With that, he went back to his car and came back with four gallons of product and put them on my desk. He said, they have four different enzyme products that they need brochures and advertising literature on and I just don't have the time or interest in doing it. Plus, that is not my area of expertise. I knew you were doing that kind of work.

I learned from him that the two he had spoken with in Las Vegas had developed a process for brewing and creating enzyme products and had a production facility in operation on the edge of Las Vegas. They had four patented products. Turfzyme was a product for the soil to enhance water absorption, stimulate and nurture grass growth and was helpful with all gardening needs. He told me that it was currently being used by most of the golf courses in Las Vegas. The second product was Enzymagic. It was a cleaning product that was currently being used by several of the casinos in Las Vegas as well as several of the car washes. The third product was Pactozyme. It was a product to add to the water when building a road in order to meet federal standards on compaction. The fourth product was Bactozyme. It was a very unique product designed for odor control, for eliminating unwanted algae in ponds, and for dispersing oil or cleaning up oil on your garage floor. Each product had just a little label identifying what it was.

After learning as much as I could from him about the products and the people in Las Vegas, I agreed to give them a call and see what we could figure out. My first impression when speaking to them was that they were in a little bit over their head. They had a tiger by the tail and didn't know whether to hang on or let go. I explained that I would need to know a lot more about their products in order to do a decent job of preparing the sales literature. That might entail coming to see their plant and meeting with them but, I believed we could help them. The result of that first conversation was my commitment to review what I had learned thus far and get back to them in a couple of days.

Before those two days were up, a tragic event in California began to dominate the news. One of Union Oil's off shore drilling platforms just outside Santa Barbara had ruptured and thousands of gallons of crude oil were being dumped into the ocean. It was being declared the worst oil spill in U.S. history. Putting two and two together, I sensed an opportunity. I called Bill Hibbard, and John Batistoni, the two inventors in Las Vegas and asked them if bactozyme might work on the oil spill in Santa Barbara. Their response was an excited yes. It's not something they had ever done, but they thought it would definitely help in the clean -up. Then I said, with your permission, I would like to try to find a way to make that happen .That permission was gladly granted.

My first call was to the office of our senior senator from Colorado, Gordon Allott. I explained that I needed to speak with the senator about an urgent matter regarding the oil spill in California. She left the phone for a minute and then came back and said, the senator can see you as soon as you can come. That was only thirty minutes. I explained to senator Allott that I was working with some people in Las Vegas that had developed a product for dispersing oil that they believed would help in the clean-up of the oil spill, and I needed an entree to Union Oil. Without hesitation, Senator Allott said, I will get you an appointment, right here in town at the Federal Center, with the EPA and the Interior Dept. You will need to convince them and they will, no doubt, need a demonstration; but, if they agree, they will send you to Union Oil. He added, God knows we need help! With that, he picked up the phone and made a call with me sitting there. The appointment was for the next morning. So, in January of 1969, I was to demonstrate a product that I had only just learned about to a group of professionals who would, no doubt, pepper me with a host of questions I might not be able to answer. At this point, my head was spinning. Perhaps, I had bitten off more than I could chew.

I went back to my office and called Las Vegas again. I told them I needed to know the best way to demonstrate their product in my meeting tomorrow. I, also, needed to know all they could tell me to be able to answer the questions I knew would be coming. I only had one gallon of the Bactozyme. They suggested I use a large vat filled with water. Get yourself a small spray gun and fill the tank with the Bactozyme. Have them spread oil in the water, a lot of oil. Then spray it with your Bactozyme and see what happens. Talk about a leap of faith. That was certainly what this was. All I knew was what I had been told, and we all know that sometimes talk is cheap. After hanging up, I called the Federal Center and asked if they had a large vat that could be used for a demonstration. They said, yes, we use one all the time in our work and we can have it set up when you come. I then set about gathering what I would need for tomorrow.

When I arrived at the Federal Center the next morning I was surprised to see no less than twenty people gathered around to witness a demonstration. A large vat of water nearly ten feet long had been set up in their work area which was ideal for the demo;

but, I had not expected such a crowd. After talking for a few minutes about the product, I took a container with about four quarts of oil and poured it into the water. The oil immediately began to spread across the entire tank. When it had completely covered the tank, I took my sprayer, and with shaky knees sprayed the entire tank with Bactozyme. There was a collective gasp from the onlookers when the oil all began to come together in one area. It didn't even look like the amount I had put in; but, it would be easy now to scoop up the remainder. They were not the only one's impressed. I was as well.

The next step was to make a presentation to Union Oil at the site of the spill. The Federal Center in Denver made the appointment. I called Las Vegas and told them what was happening and asked them to ship several barrels of Bactozyme to Santa Barbara in care of Union Oil post haste. They agreed and sent it priority shipping. I flew to Los Angeles and rented a van for the drive to Santa Barbara. In Los Angeles, I rented a large spray gun and headed up the coast. When I arrived there, the Bactozyme had not yet arrived, but the shipping company assured us it would be there early next morning. That day at my appointment, I was greeted by three of Union Oil's research and development people; but, not one executive spokesperson for Union Oil. They were full of questions. How does it work? Why does it work? What's in it? Utilizing only the information gathered from my phone conversations, I answered each of their questions the best I could. The one about, what's in it, was left unanswered. I explained, it is a patented product and while I can tell you all the ingredients are natural and safe, the ingredients are proprietary.

The next morning, the three Union Oil people and I were at the pier in Santa Barbara harbor along with two Union Oil laborers to wrestle the barrels. Using a small craft we went a short distance into the harbor. The oil from the spill had already entered the harbor and was beginning to mess up the beaches. They stopped the boat and allowed the wake to settle, then the two workers for

Union Oil using my sprayer began spreading Bactozyme on the harbor. It did exactly what it had done in Denver. I could tell, the Union Oil people were impressed. They said, we need to get back and talk with management. The demonstration was cut short, and we headed back. Another appointment was set for the next day.

The next morning, I met with some lower level executives for Union Oil. It was apparent from the minute the interview began there was some tension between the execs and the research team. One of the execs said, our people should never have allowed you to do a demonstration on the harbor. We have the EPA on our backs all the time with environmental concerns, and we know nothing about your product. We need to see the documentation that shows it would be safe on the environment and not kill the kelp and other marine life. I repeated my claim that it was all natural ingredients. It would be safe for the environment. He responded, prove it to me. That prompted a call to Las Vegas to the patent holders. They had to admit that those studies had not been done because they had considered them unnecessary. I pointed out that it was the EPA and the Interior Department that sent me, but that fell on deaf ears. My little adventure with Union Oil was over.

This story has a very interesting postscript. Union Oil ended up using their own product called Correxit on the oil spill. By using their own product, they were able to mitigate some of the cost of the loss from the spill and I suspect there were tax credits as well. The part that is difficult for this mind to comprehend is knowing that Correxit is toxic. It did kill the kelp and marine life. The same product was used for both the Valdez oil spill in Alaska and the disastrous spill in the Caribbean more recently. The lawsuits for the damage done by Correxit in the Valdez spill are still in court to the day of this writing. I leave it to my reader to figure that one out.

Leaving Santa Barbara and Los Angeles, I flew directly to Las Vegas to meet the owners of Nevada Enzymes, the company manufacturing the products. Once there I learned that the three principals were Bill Hibbard, and John Battistoni, the patent holders, and Bill Crawford, a Las Vegas attorney that had led them through the patent process and had subsequently become an officer in the corporation. They had been struggling for two or three years trying to get marketing going beyond the local market. In listening to what they had been doing, it looked like the blind leading the blind. While some of their ideas had been productive, such as getting some famous people like Arthur Godfrey to use their product and give them endorsement letters, the overall effort had been sadly lacking.

The end result of that first meeting was a signed contract written up by their attorney granting me full world-wide marketing rights to all of their products. I had promised them an aggressive marketing plan that would include individual franchises in markets all around the world. It was my intention to give it to them. I flew back to Denver with the contract in my pocket. This new venture was going to require a new corporation. My attorney formed the corporation, Enzymatic International, with the allowance for limited shares to be sold according to Colorado law. This would give us the funding we needed for the initial startup. It was set up to allow for the possibility of a later public offering. I was the President. My Vice President was a former Colonel in the army who had a great deal of marketing savvy as well as a lot of good contacts. He was also a major investor. The rest of the board included some of the investors along with some that had a vested interest in the environment. Enzyme products were at that time in the forefront of the environmental movement.

From the first day, we decided to move the marketing forward in several different directions at the same time. For marketing product in the local region, we hired salesmen, on commission, and my brother, Robert became sales manager for the Colorado area. His efforts turned up an interesting prospect in the form of Gates Rubber Company. Gates was at that time one of the larger companies in Denver. While their primary business was manufacturing tires, they had their fingers in many pies. One of the most interesting to me was a large research and development department investigating the use of enzymes. They also had a large pig farm in Longmont that had a huge odor problem. The neighbors from miles around had been complaining about the odors emanating from their holding pond. Robert sold them many barrels of Bactozyme to spray on their pond. The odor problem was solved. In just a matter of days, Gates Rubber Company called and wanted to talk to me. The subsequent conversations revealed a strong interest in becoming a partner in this new venture. They were interested in a merger in which they would own 51 percent of the company, but they would become the research and development operation and would provide the funding for doing the research that had been so sadly neglected by those in Las Vegas. Gates was a multi-million dollar corporation and this would assure our success. It was my reasoning that it would be much better to be a smaller part of a successful company than the many risks involved with a start-up company. My board agreed.

A meeting was set with Nevada Enzymes and the scientists from Gates flew to Las Vegas with me. Once there, the Las Vegan group gave us all a tour of their plant and the large vats where the products were being produced. Later came the negotiations. While the Gates people were pleased with everything they had seen, the primary sticking point was access to the patents which would reveal the ingredients. The Gates people argued that no company is going to risk millions of dollars without being able to review the patents. Bill Hibbard and John Battistoni were adamant that if they revealed their patents, Gates could steal what they had been spending years to develop. Their suspicion reached the level of paranoia. I explained that there were legal safeguards that could prevent that from happening, and I agreed that no company was likely to make a large commitment without that. The end result was Gates being rebuffed. On the way back to Denver, I had opportunity to talk some more with the Gates scientists. They said their analysis of the Bactozyme revealed an extraordinary enzyme activity but, they were very disappointed with the results of our meeting. I acknowledged that I, too, was very disappointed, but we would continue working with them on their in house needs and providing product for both their pig farm and their cattle feed yard.

Meanwhile, the local marketing was coming along. The salesmen had carwashes around town using Enzymagic and turf farms using Turfzyme. Garden shops were selling Turfzyme in gallons for home use but, everywhere we turned we ran into the same problem. Where is the research showing that the products are really safe? Can we be assured there are no carcinogens or other cancer causing ingredients? The need for that research was becoming more obviously apparent, and for that we were talking really big bucks. The local activity had created a sufficient hubbub that it warranted a visit from the EPA. They made it clear that the research needed to be done.

We decided to take another stab at finding a company for a merger. My Vice President had a good friend on the board of Chemagro in Kansas City. They were a wholly owned subsidiary of Bayer, the megalith German company that produces Bayer Aspirin and hundreds of other products. That contact led to a meeting in Kansas City with Chemagro and Bayer. Again we all made the trip to Las Vegas. Bayer made all kinds of overtures, including a trip to Germany for all of the principals of Nevada Enzymes and myself, to see their laboratory and meet their research people. However, they demanded the same thing as Gates had. I expected it, but I hoped the Las Vegas people would now see the wisdom of such a merger. Their paranoia persisted. Another rebuff. It was becoming apparent that they were not going to budge, and we were going to be limited in our ability to market to major retailers. We were going to have to work with what we had and try to skirt around the EPA's concerns.

In the following months we had inquiries from no less than six other major companies who were interested in a possible merger, but every one of them had the same requirement, as I knew they would have, and each time the patent holders said no. One of the markets where we didn't have to worry about the EPA was the international market. We were successful in selling a franchise to a Jewish business man from Johannesburg, South Africa, for all of South Africa. The plant in Nevada had the largest shipment in their history on the way to the Dark Continent.

I began to believe that what was needed, in lieu of any cooperation from Nevada on the EPA concerns, was some political clout that might be an avenue to the products being accepted as they were. A call to Senator Canon, the senior senator from Nevada, got some immediate results. An appointment was made in his office for John Battistoni to talk to him about the possibility of an entree into the GSA, the office for government purchases. I told John to point out to the senator that the Atomic Energy Commission had been unable to meet the compaction standards on their road to the Nevada test site until they used our product Pactozyme and then they met the standard easily. Explain to him the issues we have been having with the EPA and seek his advice.

The Nevada meeting resulted in an invitation to Washington, D.C. extended by Senator Canon. John Battistoni and I flew to Washington. We had decided to go one day early in order to kill two birds with one stone. We had been communicating with Arthur Godfrey whose Beacon Hill Farm was just over the border from Washington in Virginia. He had used our Bactozyme in his chick sills at his retreat in Idaho on the Snake River. For the uninitiated a chick sill is the gentleman's name for an outhouse. He had been very pleased with the result, but he was having a big problem with algae at his Beacon Hill Farm. When we knew we were coming to Washington, John Battistoni offered to spray his pond. Arthur Godfrey was a big star at that time, and he believed it would be good publicity. We rented the spray equipment in Washington and drove to Beacon Hill Farm. We had the product shipped ahead. When we arrived there, Mr. Godfrey was in the corral working with his trick horse, Goldie. If you have ever seen any of the old Arthur Godfrey shows you have seen Goldie. Arthur's wife was in the skating rink that he had especially built for his Olympic star wife. After introducing ourselves and visiting for a few minutes, we went to the pond to spray. It was totally clogged with algae. Fortunately, even though it was winter, we had caught a warm day. Enzymes require an ambient temperature that is fairly warm in order to be active. We gave the pond a good spraying, said our farewells and asked Arthur to let us know how his pond fared. We learned later that he was pleased with the result. Other than a letter from him telling of his experience with the product, I'm not aware of any great benefit that came from that effort.

Back in Washington, John and I went out to a good Washington dinner and talked about our strategy for the next day. That morning we were somewhat surprised when we were picked up at the hotel by a limousine and two of Senator Canon's aides. We were expecting to be meeting with someone from the GSA, but instead we were driven to the senate office building. The aides said, there is someone here you need to meet. They got us seated in the cafeteria of the Senate Office Building. What happened next is totally bizarre. A huge African American man came in and sat down at our table. Without saying a word, he took a wad of bills out of his pocket and began going through it. As he did, he said, I don't like the tens and the twenties. I like the fifties and the hundreds. Sitting there, pretty much dumb struck, we waited for him to continue. I understand you have products you would like to sell to the Federal Government. I am here to make that happen for you. I am part of a public relations firm in Harrisburg, Penn. that assists start-up companies like yours to get a foothold with government purchases. You need to come with me to Harrisburg to meet the other principals. With that, he got up and left. Still totally confused, we spoke further to Senator Canon's aides. They explained that the man we had just met had been President Nixon's point man for getting out the black vote in Pennsylvania during the 1968 election. He and his firm handled purchases to the government. We needed to go meet them in Harrisburg. We went back to our hotel. I was having great misgivings about this trip and thought, maybe, we should just go back to Denver. John, however, thought we needed to follow-up and see what might happen. Somewhat reluctantly, I agreed.

The next morning we were picked up again and told a meeting had been set at the Senate Bar and Grill in Harrisburg for lunch. With that, Senator Canon's aides excused themselves saying they had other business they needed to attend to, but the driver would get us there and then back to Washington. It was pretty drive, even in winter, but as John and I sat in the back of the limo and conversed quietly between ourselves, I was not feeling comfortable; but, I decided to keep my feelings to myself. At the luncheon we met the two principals. They bought us a nice lunch and then launched into their sales pitch. They names company after company that they represented and what they had done for them. After lunch, they asked us to accompany them to the Pennsylvania State Warehouse right there in Harrisburg. Once there we walked right past the guard and receptionist with just a nod and a wave from our hosts. They, obviously were well known. Once inside, they showed us one section that contained the product from one of their clients. It was lead free paint. There was enough lead free paint in that warehouse to paint every building in the State of Pennsylvania. That uneasy feeling in the pit of my stomach was beginning to emerge again. When we had been at lunch, several state senators from Pennsylvania had come in. They were in special session just across the street because the state was facing possible bankruptcy and that had been the headline story in the Harrisburg papers. I thought, no wonder they are facing bankruptcy if what I am seeing is common.

After completing our tour of the state warehouse and the warehouse for the city of Harrisburg, we went back to their office for further talks. Once there, they gave us their final spiel. They explained that they had knowledge of the fact that President Nixon was going to appoint a new head of the Government Purchasing

Office, and that he was going to appoint a second in command who was going to be their man. This was going to happen in the next thirty days. They would then have total access. They assured us that we would have orders for product that would put our company on the map. They went on to explain that they already controlled a lot of the purchasing for both New Jersey and New York. Both states, by the way, that were in financial trouble as well. Then came their final pitch. They needed a good will payment up front in the amount of $10,000 dollars. Then we were to give them a contract granting them exclusive control over all purchases made by the Federal Government. They would receive a 15% commission off the top. I explained that I would have to consult with my board, but I will get back to you. On the ride back to Washington, John was lobbying hard that we should take the deal. I told him there was no way I could take that back to my board and recommend that we do it. I thought the whole thing reeked of corruption and we should stay clear.

As a postscript to this story, I would like to point to two salient facts. At the time, Senator Canon was the Republican head of the senate ethics committee. Ironic? While the Nevada people were quite unhappy with me for turning down the deal, I felt I was exonerated only two years later when an FBI investigation resulted in the arrest and charging of several people in the Harrisburg operation, and the head two people in the Government Purchasing Office as well. It is interesting to note that these investigations seldom lead to the head of the snake. It seems that this is what we have come to expect in our government. I truly wish it wasn't so.

After returning from Washington, we made a number of other efforts to get marketing started, but our options were becoming more limited, and we continued to be hounded by the lack of research that had been done. Local marketing had slowed to a crawl and most of the salesmen had moved on to greener pastures. Only Robert and one other remained, and Robert was under financial pressure at home. The corporation had maxed out its borrowing capability and had looming debt that was going to be difficult if not impossible to meet. The end result was predictable. There was no choice but to file for chapter seven bankruptcy. Enzymatic International Corporation ceased to exist. I later learned that John Battistoni and his associates took the name International Enzymes and continued their operation in Nevada.

This story ends as you might expect. Greed never turns out well. Nevada Enzymes sat on their patents and continued their feeble efforts. As you know, patents only remain proprietary for seven years. After seven years, the patents became public. When John Batistoni died in March of 2019, he left behind a company with four employees and a gross annual sales volume of less than $800,000. That is about what they had in the 1970's.Meanwhile, the products are being produced all over the world. Bactosyme is popular in India, and Enzymagic is readily available on Amazon. What should have been a multi-million dollar mega-corporation is relegated to the back waters of history.

This entire episode left me in a state of emotional trauma. Most of the people who had trusted me and relied on my judgment were people I loved or at least cared deeply about. They were my friends. While not one single person expressed incriminations against me for what had happened, I still felt responsible. Some of them had lost a good deal of money. It was time for me to take a hard look at my life and what I had become. It was a far cry from what I had set out to be. As I began to gather my thoughts and look at what I still had going with the little ad agency, I received a call from the one who had been my mentor during college, Rev. Walter Jewett. Walter was retired now and was living in Sun City Arizona. I had visited him there while on a marketing trip for Enzymatic International. He had been very cordial, but had expressed grave concern over the fact that I was out of Christian work. I explained to him I would love to be back doing God's work, but I had strong feelings about doing it as a divorced man. It did not seem appropriate to me. It was left at that point. Walter's call today was to tell me that he had been praying hard over my issue. He went on to say that scripture makes allowance for divorce in cases of infidelity and besides, he felt I was selling God short in not allowing for redemption. He said, Rex, have you really asked God to forgive you for the choices you have made and their consequence. He related to me again the story of David and Bathsheba. He said, I think you owe it to yourself to speak with the Bishop for Colorado and seek his counsel.

After a number of highly personal prayer sessions, I felt a burden being lifted from my heart. It was with a sense of eager enthusiasm that I called and made an appointment with the Bishop. It had been a number of years since I had felt this good. The Bishop listened patiently as I related all the history of my past. I left nothing out. When I was done, he made a couple of calls to verify my credentials and then said, Rex, I have the ideal spot for you. We have a church in Southern Colorado that has just lost their pastor. It is a nice church in a very nice community. It is a two point charge. Walsh Methodist Church has the parsonage and you would also be covering Two Buttes Methodist Church with a 9:30 service. If you choose to accept, you could begin as early as next week. I said I was very inclined to say yes, but I needed to discuss it with my wife and family and I would get back to him in a couple of days.

There was some reticence on Margaret's part. She had never planned on being a preacher's wife. While she shared my religious values, she didn't know if she could fill the role she would be expected to play. Would the people accept her? Would they understand that she had no specific training for this? Could she adjust to this new responsibility? I assured her that people would love her just the way she was. She was a genuine and compassionate person and I knew, without doubt, that people would love her. After we had talked about it, I called the Bishop and said, yes. I gave what remained of our ad agency to Nan, packed all of our furniture into a moving van, and with Margaret following in the car, we headed for Walsh. My life was about to make a 380 degree turn.

9

Following My Heart

IT WAS LATE EVENING WHEN OUR LITTLE CARAVAN arrived in Walsh. We drove to the back of the parsonage to begin unloading. We had been told the door would be open. As we began getting out of the car, the carillon bells in the church tower began to ring. One of the children said, Dad, they are welcoming you to Walsh. My silent prayer of thanksgiving would confirm that I shared the feeling. First impressions are always important, and in this case, the first impression of the entire family was positive. The parsonage was large and the appliances nearly new. A quick trip over to the church to see my office and the interior of the sanctuary with its beautiful stained glass windows left me wondering how such a pretty church with its tall steeple and carillon bells was built in this small rural community. Over the next two and one half years, all those questions would be answered.

My first Sunday was a memorable one. I felt it necessary to share with my congregation enough of my history to explain where I had been for the years out of the pulpit. As I did, I could see many in the congregation that told me by their response that they had been there and done that. The general feeling was empathetic. I don't recall my scripture lesson for that day. All of my services in Walsh were recorded, so I have the record somewhere. Following the service was a pot-luck dinner in our honor. I don't recall ever having a pot-luck dinner in any one of my churches where everyone stayed. This time, I saw no one leave. Everyone stayed. By the time we left the church and returned to the parsonage, Margaret knew she was accepted as was I. There is no greater feeling than the one of acceptance. The children had already found a group of new friends that promised to introduce them at school and their smiles told us they were excited and pleased. As I returned to my office later, for a time of solitude and prayer, my heart was full, and the emotion almost overwhelming. For the first time, in a very long time, I felt like I was home. I would have been content to remain right here for the rest of my life.

Walsh turned out to be a rural farming community. Wheat was the number one crop, but followed closely by broomcorn. Walsh was the largest producer of broomcorn in Colorado. Large storage facilities were used for the broomcorn. The town had four large grain storage bins for wheat, all owned by the Thompson family who were also members of the church. Cattle were right up there, as well. The Thompson's had a large feed lot where they fattened cattle for market. One of our members was Hugh Schooley. He owned and operated the local grocery store. It would be only a short time before Margaret made the decision to help out. She hooked up with Hugh and went to work stocking groceries.

For me, Walsh was like a dream come true. It put me right back where I had spent all my young life. Walsh was noted for the flights of northern Canadian geese that flocked to this area. Half way between Walsh and Two Buttes was a place called Turks Lake. Thousands of greater and lesser northern geese flew into there each day. It was not long before I had my shotgun out and was making a trip once a week to hunt geese. Margaret soon had more geese in the freezer than she had room. She said, no more. She found some very creative ways to fix a goose dinner. The area was also prime hunting for pheasant, grouse, and quail in season. Oh, and did I forget, the fishing was great. I was content.

The work in the church was going very well. I found myself spending an inordinate amount of my time in pastoral counseling. The congregation seemed to sense that my life experience somehow made me more qualified to help them with their real life issues than someone who had never experienced any of those issues. I, myself, wonder at times how a priest who has never been married or others whose lives have been pristine can comprehend some of the issues faced by their flock. That counseling included quite a number of our youth. Margaret had fit right in, helping to lead the ladies fellowship. I had been confident she would. Margaret had come from a Lutheran background, but her confirmation and experience in the church gave her qualifications that even she did not know she had. She was content, as well.

In our first year, the church decided to host a Lay Witness Mission. People from churches as far away as Western Kansas came to be a part of it. We had some well-known speakers of that era booked as guests. It was at this mission that my son, Drew, gave his heart to Christ. He remembers it as a great spiritual experience. On the second day of the mission, Margret and I had to go into Springfield where the hospital was located. It was a last minute trip and we were in a bit of a hurry. Driving into town we were following a pick-up pulling a trailer filled with bags of trash. A large pipe fell off the truck in front of our car. I instinctively swerved to avoid it and lost control of the automobile. When we hit the ditch it caused the car to overturn. Two flips later we ended up in the field, having just missed the light pole. We were transported to the hospital for X-rays and treatment. Fortunately, neither of us had any broken bones. We were very stiff and sore, but we both made it to that evening's service, although we were late coming in midway through the service. We were greeted by applause and surrounded by the love of a caring congregation who offered up prayers of thanksgiving on our behalf. We both remember that day with hearts that are still grateful for our deliverance from what could have been terminal for both of us. Another example of Divine Providence?

There were literally hundreds of things that occurred during these years that I could point to as memorable, but I will only speak of a few and those not necessarily in the order or sequence of when they occurred. It was during this time that Tony became very active in sports. Walsh was the defending state champion in high school football, so Tony played football, but he preferred wrestling. He was small in stature and in wrestling you always compete at your weight level. He was 119 pounds and built much like his father back in my high school years. We spent a good deal of time following him to tournaments around the area. As a freshman he went to the state tournament and took second place. He was pinned in his finals match.

One of the summers, the boy's went to a church camp near the Air Force Academy. While there, Tony found a wounded sparrow hawk. We always speculated that it was one being trained by someone from the Academy. They trained falcons and other hawks as well. Tony brought him home and nursed him back to health. We got a large cage for him and hung it on our tree in the backyard. Margaret's mother had already passed away, and her dad was in poor health. The family was taking turns in having Dad come to live for three months at a time. He came for his three month stay in Walsh. Every day, Pop would sit on the back patio and watch that sparrow hawk. He would mention regularly that this was his favorite place to be. I'm sure it reminded him of the farm and his youth. He, also, loved Margaret's cooking. One day we went into the backyard and the sparrow hawk was gone. I know Pop let him go but, all he said was, somebody must have left the cage door open. Bless his heart, he knew that sparrow hawk deserved to be free.

When Tony was in eighth grade he surprised us and made us all proud. The high school science teacher was also teacher for the eighth grade. Each year, he took his best science students to Oklahoma State University's summer seminar and the accompanying science test. This year he came to me and asked for permission for Tony to go along. He felt it would be good experience and Tony was his star pupil in science. We willing gave our permission. When they arrived home we learned that Tony, as an eighth grader, had scored the highest accumulated score in the history of the school. Needless to say, his popularity in school skyrocketed. He was always well liked by the other students, but now he had some additional standing. All of the children loved Walsh. As I was writing this, my son, Drew was quick to point out that everything was not always rosy for him at Walsh. He became good friends with John, the Baptist preacher's son. John was always in trouble, and he and Drew, managed to find some of that together.

Somewhere we acquired a beautiful German shepherd dog we called Fritz. He was king of the neighborhood, and a friend to all the little old ladies. The boys spent many hours out in the fields hunting with Fritz. He was very fast and more than a match for most of the rabbits. Great fun for growing boys but, Fritz was destined to do one bad thing that would come back to bite us later. Hugh Schooley had a pedigreed English bulldog that was show quality and he had planned to breed him to another show dog in La Junta. He had a high fenced yard, but when his bulldog came into season that fence didn't stop Fritz. Hugh found him in the yard and knew it was too late to do anything about it. He brought Fritz home and was obviously not pleased. Who could blame him? To hear the rest of the story, you will have to read further on.

We had only been in Walsh for two and one-half years when the Bishop called me in and said I needed to be closer to Denver, so I could return to school. He told me he was going to appoint me to Simla and Matheson which were forty miles east of Colorado Springs on the highway to Limon. I understood, but I can't say I was pleased. I told you earlier that when I was in the Catskills of New York, I had the feeling I would be content there for the rest of my life. I had that same feeling about Walsh. It was very difficult for the children. They had really settled into the community and they felt they were abandoning all their friends. In late June, after Annual Conference, we moved to Simla.

In many ways, Simla was like culture shock. They were a small community, but close enough to Colorado Springs to be affected by the city culture. Drugs were a problem and I immediately found this to be something I was going to have to deal with. The culture with the kids seemed poles apart from Walsh. The sense of permissiveness was apparent. Walsh high school had been very active with the Fellowship of Christian Athletes in the sports programs and coaches gave great leadership to the kids. While there, the Fellowship sponsored a charity basketball game between the locals and the Denver Bronco Basketball team. The locals were the first to beat the Bronco's. In Simla, I'm not certain the coach was even a Christian and there were several activists in the community actively fighting the separation of church and state issue. It was not long before I learned there was a coven of witches in town as well as a group of Devil worshipers. I never knew exactly who it was, but I had my suspicions.

My predecessor had been a lady pastor. While I never knew her, I'm certain she was a fine person, but the church had been allowed to just coast. Part of that was because the older congregation felt the world was passing them by and they simply wanted to retreat into their own reality. The congregation was not large, but they were faithful, loyal Christians who just felt they had been betrayed by a new world order they could not comprehend. They had lost their Evangelical zeal and had pretty much stopped reaching out. The school was quite secular. When I gave the graduation address to the senior class two years later, I remember being cautioned about my prayer. I ignored that, but I did hear some carping about the mentioning of Jesus.

My enrollment in Iliff School of Theology on the campus of the University of Denver was completed in time for the fall semester. It was a difficult schedule, but doable. I would spend Monday through Thursday in the dorm at Iliff, then home till Monday. Our professors were great and I was deeply enmeshed. It was good to get back to scholarly pursuits even though it presented many hardships, not the least of which was financial. Over the next two years that condition would continue to exacerbate. Between the cost of school and the demands of the family, our budget was being taxed to the limit. My salary at Simla was only $10,000.00 a year. It was not long before Margaret was noticing that the money wasn't stretching. She was doing all she could. She was again working for the local grocery store, but at minimum wage. Even minimum wage nearly matched what I was earning. Not that I deserved more than that being at school four days a week. Margaret's talents were far greater than minimum wage, but with me gone, she needed to be in Simla for the children, and there was simply no other employment available. Good employment was a one hundred mile a day round trip and that was just not feasible.

It didn't happen right away, but at some point during our second year, I decided to try supplementing my income by going to the track some during the week. When I had gone to watch Cliff's horses run, I had been quite successful in my handicapping. At that time I was not under the gun financially. It was more for fun. Now, it was serious. It is much harder when you need to win. Your decision making is impaired by odds and other factors that should not be part of the handicapping process. To make that worse, I discovered that there was a dog track in town, and you could bet on the greyhounds. Some Friday's I would go home and give Margaret several hundred dollars from that week's gambling. Other weeks, I had to tell her that our grocery budget for the week was shot. One week I gave her a check for over three thousand dollars from an exotic bet. It was those weeks that fueled the desire to continue on. I had a bit of a problem with my conscience over my gambling, but when we want to rationalize something, we will always find a way. In this case, I rationalized that the church had given tacit approval to what I was doing. The majority owner and President of

Centennial Race Track was Richard Simon. He was, also, chairman of the Board of Trustee's for Iliff School of Theology. Is that not tacit approval? I will be talking about that in my final chapter. Let me just say here that we are all responsible for the decisions we make and pawning off that responsibility to someone else just doesn't work.

A lot of other things happened at Simla that are worth mentioning. It was here that the Sample family was able to put together a little musical group. Tony played lead guitar, I played rhythm guitar, Alexis played guitar and later on stand-up base and we all sang. On our first Christmas at Simla, we jointly wrote original music for the Christmas story and presented it in church. Margaret did the narration and the rest of us sang, even little Terri, who was still quite young. Our little group gained enough recognition to be asked to perform for the County Fair in Kiowa and other functions in the area such as Cowboy Camp. We continued to perform together until the time Tony fell victim to brain cancer.

One of the more humorous things that happened at Simla occurred on a Sunday in our first year. Church was just letting out and our new German shepherd was greeting everyone as they came out the door. Fritz had been hit by a car and killed shortly before leaving Walsh, and we had found another German shepherd who was even much nicer than Fritz. This one actually would walk the little old ladies that lived up the hill all the way to the grocery store downtown. They all loved him and they would find excuses to walk downtown so he would accompany them. He was a fortunate addition to the family. On this Sunday ... began to bark and headed toward the parsonage next door. When we looked there was a covered pickup in our driveway and the garage door was open. As we approached, a smiling Hugh Schooley stepped out of the garage. He said, well, your dog sired them so you can find a home for them. He had brought us five of the ugliest puppies you have ever seen. Anyone who thinks a bulldog and a shepherd would make cute pups needs to think again. Hugh thought it was great fun and also poetic justice. He stayed for dinner and filled us in on all the news from Walsh; but, we had the responsibility for finding homes for all those pups just old enough to wean. That turned out to be easier than we expected. I guess ugly is cute to some.

The boys continued their participation in sports. They both played football and Drew played basketball as well. As an eighth grader his squad was selected to play in a tournament at the Air Force Academy. The tournament included teams from AAA, AA, and A schools. Simla was an A school. The A schools were really just cannon fodder for the larger schools and not expected to do much. Simla ended up beating them all. Drew was high scoring center for the tournament. Even though there were some successes and some high points, the boys' high school experience in sports was not what it could have been. They didn't like the coaches or their attitude and this was something that was felt by most of the team. Tony, also, had the misfortune of dropping a pass in the end zone on the final play of a crucial play -off game. That dropped pass haunted him for years. I think Simla had the talent to be state champions if they had the coaches from Walsh. Just my opinion.

Drew spent his summer's working on the farm for one of the members of the Matheson Church. Tony worked for the State Conservation District in Ramah. Margaret continued working for the grocery store, but added the job of cleaning and servicing the rooms at the local motel. That one ate my heart out. I was reaching a crisis point in my thinking. We were approaching a new year when the Bishop would be making his appointments. I feared my indebtedness was soon going to become an embarrassment to the church if collections came in against my salary. I went to the Bishop and told him I was going to be forced to take secular employment in order to take care of my financial obligations. I explained that I expected my indebtedness could become embarrassing to the church. He agreed and our tenure at Simla was about to end. While there are always some in a church fellowship that you will miss and some that will always fill a special place in your heart, my over-all experience at Simla, I would rate as the lowest in my ministerial career. I empathize with the pastors in some of the inner city churches and what they have to deal with in today's world. I had only experienced the fringes of it in Simla, but looking forward, the erosion of our culture and values is frightening. We continue to be in need of a great revival. Hopefully, more Billy Graham's will appear on the horizon.

We were, once again, leaving my chosen career, and my passion, to work in the secular world. While I still harbor some regrets that I was unable to figure out a different answer, I remain confident that family comes first. It would be a long time before I would have another opportunity.

10

When Family Comes First

MY DECISION TO LEAVE SIMLA HAD BEEN A DIFFICULT one, and was prompted by a growing sense of desperation. Some of what had happened was totally my fault and I was suffering the consequences of my bad decisions. Yet, much of it was the result of circumstances that were beyond my control. The bottom line was that I now needed some immediate action to alleviate the situation. We moved to Colorado Springs and I began seeking employment. I took the first job that was offered on the very first day. On Sunday, I had been in the pulpit. On Tuesday, I began driving a Yellow Cab in Colorado Springs.

Working for Yellow Cab turned out to be more profitable then I had expected at first. The salary wasn't anything to crow about, but the opportunity for good tips was up to the individual driver. Good service and going beyond what might normally be expected of a cab driver resulted in better tips. The job, also, quickly became almost a pastoral job. Who ever heard of a Yellow Cab driver being a counselor? Answer: someone who has never driven a Yellow Cab. The variety of people I carried was almost too diverse to cover. There were White House personnel going to conferences at the

Broadmoor Hotel, International diplomats, traveling salesmen, and ordinary vacationers and tourists; many from foreign countries, especially Japan. I found them all interesting, and most of them wanting to visit and ask questions. Tourists would ask about the best restaurants, salesmen the best night clubs. When I was on the night shift, there would be multiple times we would be called for someone who was inebriated and needing a ride home. The night shift always put you in touch with the seamier side of life. More than once, I found myself trying to find shelter for young runaways from home that found themselves on the street with no place to go. My contacts with the church gave me resources to place them out of harm's way. It would be safe to say that I was enjoying my work and finding it more rewarding than I had expected, but I knew it was only temporary.

Meanwhile, Margaret had found good employment with Sunburst Pattern Company. She was now earning a decent wage and between us we were already on the road to financial recovery. I had put my resume out to a variety of places including the employment agencies because of my history in Chicago and New York. The largest one in Colorado Springs called me in for interview. After some negotiation, I agreed to leave Yellow Cab and return to a field that I knew and understood, even though it had never been one that I could say I truly enjoyed. There were parts of it that were rewarding. Meeting new people and helping them to improve their lives by job advancement, then seeing their excitement when it all came together was rewarding. But, the day to day grind of seeking new job listings and finding new clients was very mundane and a little boring. I did it because the pay was good and that was important.

It was less than a year later when Margaret said, there may be a spot for me with Sunburst Pattern Company. They are going to hire a new lecturer and I think it might be something you would find interesting. You need to know just what Sunburst Pattern Company did and what Margaret was doing for them. Two design people had created a system for making patterns that was patented and had evolved into a business. They had lecturers covering the entire country. The method of operation was quite simple. A lecturer would be scheduled into a town for a meeting. His coming would be advertised for a month prior in the newspapers and local media. The appeal was to all those who did their own sewing and made their own clothes. There was a $10.00 charge for the class. It was usually held at a local hotel meeting room or a larger venue if the anticipated attendance warranted it. On the week of the meeting, Margret would find a local television station that did a ladies daytime show and schedule the Sunburst lecturer to appear on live T.V. and do a demonstration of making a pattern. This always elicited a good response. The class itself covered a lot of the basics of making your own clothes and then a demonstration of how easy it was to create a pattern that would fit perfectly on any figure. Getting a proper fit is the challenge for all home seamstresses, especially pants. A volunteer model would be selected from the audience. Everyone expected you to select someone with that perfect, easy to fit figure but, instead, the lecturer would ask for a model that had difficulty getting a proper fit. The overweight or even obese, or someone with large thighs who couldn't make pants that fit would be the choice for the lecturer. When he was able to make a sloper for a pattern that fit perfectly, it was like turning on a light for the real sewers. At the end of the class, the pattern book containing hundreds of patented patterns and the tools for making them were made available for sale. There was a follow-up customer service for anyone who had difficulty and needed additional help. This was a call-in service.

This sounded interesting enough to merit a second look. Margaret introduced me to Connie Brooks, her boss and President of the company. I explained to him that I knew absolutely nothing about sewing. Some of his lecturers were graduates from design school or professional pattern makers. I was none of those things. Mr. Brooks said, don't let that concern you. We can teach you everything you need to know, and we think someone who is not a professional may be more effective speaking with amateur seamstresses than a professional. He said, Margaret had filled him in on the things I had done and he was willing to take a chance on me if I was willing to give it a try. I guess I have always been a sucker for a challenge. This would certainly be that. The temptation was too great to resist. I said, yes.

The next few weeks were like going back to school all over again. I began to learn about sewing and pattern making. I learned tips on sewing shortcuts and how to correct and alter a garment that didn't fit. I listened to dozens of recorded lectures from the classes of other lecturers. In thirty days, Connie thought I was ready for a trial run. They had advertised my coming to Raton, New Mexico and had booked me at the Best Western Hotel. On the day of that first lecture, I was a nervous jenny. Was I really ready? When I walked into the meeting room it was empty, but it was early. Soon people began arriving. By the time it was ready to start over fifty people were in attendance. To my surprise, the lecture and demonstration went better than I had expected. I was able to answer the questions that were asked and the pattern I made fit the model perfectly. As I was giving the final presentation with the pattern book and the tools for sale, I saw Connie Brooks walk into the back of the room. He had driven down to be there for that first lecture. When nearly twenty of the women came up to purchase the system, Connie came up to help me write up the orders. When everyone was gone, Connie said, well, Rex, you are on your way.

Over the next two years, I traveled all of the Western States and as far east as Indiana. During that time, Margaret had me booked on many live television shows. The ones in San Diego and Los Angeles and Chicago are all memorable. One of the most rewarding times was a road trip we made to Texas. Margaret had me booked for lectures all across Texas. We took the whole family and for a full month we traveled together taking in the sights by day with me lecturing at night. My children remember that trip with a special fondness. By this time, I had gained enough notoriety that I would find professional pattern makers in my class there to learn from me.

One incident that stands out in my memory occurred in Provo, Utah. At the end of the lecture, and after I had finished writing up the orders, a woman came up to me along with her daughter. She explained that her daughter had been selected to be rodeo queen for the Utah State Fair, and she needed to design a couple of outfits especially for that occasion and If I would be willing to do the patterns she would gladly pay me whatever it would cost. I explained to her that I was a pattern maker, but I had no experience as a designer. All I was capable of doing was the basic patterns and slopers. Also, I needed to be in Salt Lake for a lecture the next day, so there wouldn't be time. She was not that easily dissuaded. She said, we could drive down to Salt Lake and you could do it during the day. It was not something that we ordinarily did. We wanted people to buy the system and make their own patterns. But, she had already done that. She just was under the gun for time and wanted to know that it would be right. Finally, I agreed. They came to the hotel in Salt Lake and I made the patterns for her outfit. She wanted to pay me for them, but, I refused. They had bought their book, I considered this to be customer service. I always wondered how she looked riding out into the arena as Miss Rodeo Queen.

The entire experience with Sunburst Pattern Company was an enjoyable one. It was different than anything I had ever done, but having become proficient at it gave me a sense of personal accomplishment that, in itself, was satisfying. Again it was not destined to last. Neither Margaret nor I really know what happened. We believe that the owners of the company became financially involved with some other projects that didn't work out. The result, however, is that out of the blue, both Margaret and I were informed that Sunburst Pattern Company was going into receivership and that we were both out of work. One day I was lecturing, the next day I was driving home without a job.

Margaret's recovery was almost immediate. She was hired by Equifax, the credit reporting agency. Her qualifications fit their profile perfectly and she went to work right away. It was a good job, and her income made it possible for me to do some looking for what I would do next. During these past few years, Nan had moved up into the mountains to Breckenridge and was working as the promotions and advertising manager for one of the large ski resorts. Her daughter Judy had lived there with her husband when she first went there, but as I told you earlier Judy and her husband had divorced and Judy had lived with us for a while in Franktown before going to California. We had remained in contact with Nan and now when she learned that I was leaving Sunburst, she came to me with a plan. She had long been dreaming of rejuvenating her television program "Little Stars". She owned the rights to both formats, "Little Stars" and "Your Big Break". She believed the time was right to make an effort to bring them back but, she did not think she had the oomph to make it happen. If I could make it happen, it would be mine. I thought it worth a try.

The way Mr. DonGarra had done it in Chicago was by bringing an entire package to WGN. That meant selling sponsors and bringing that presold package to the station. They didn't have to worry about getting their advertising sold. Mr. DonGarra, being in the advertising business, was able to do that effectively and that was why his show had such a long run on WGN. We decided to try to duplicate that method in Denver. In Chicago, the main sponsors had been a chain of dry cleaning companies and a major modeling school. In Denver, we ran into all kinds of skepticism about the shows viability. We were making little headway with potential sponsors, or with Channel Two, which was the sister station to WGN in Chicago. Finally, we decided to produce a one hour special, sell the advertising for just that one show and let it be a showcase that would hopefully generate the interest we were expecting.

The call went out for auditions of young talent all across the state of Colorado. The response was excellent and in a very short time we had all the talent we needed. We set about designing the show. "Little Stars" had never had its own theme song, so I wrote original music and lyrics for a theme song. We hired a man as music director for the show that had been music director on many major television shows. He put together the band. Alexis had been attending high school at Wasson in Colorado Springs and was very active in theatre. As a part of one of her programs, she and I had written a skit with all original music based on the story of Alice in Wonderland. With us it was Alice in Toyland. We had a special song for the dolly, the ballerina, the dancing panda, and the skit ended with the singing of "Over The Rainbow". We decided to incorporate that into our special. The children that were competing on the show would all come together in the end and work together with the skit and the closing song. The young girl that played Alice was in my opinion even better than Judy Garland. I knew she would be a tear jerker.

We had made arrangements to film the special at the Broadmoor in Colorado Springs. A television production company from Denver brought their truck to Colorado Springs for the filming. That all went off without a hitch. The competition portion of the show was to be shot at the studio in Denver. What we had filmed in Colorado Springs had been the special music. The show opened with shots of Pikes Peak and a narration of America the Beautiful and then all the children singing a compilation of songs ending with the theme song from "Paint Your Wagon". It ended with the Alice in Toyland skit, and then everybody singing the "Little Stars" theme song. We were all pleased with the final product. The show aired on Channel Two in Denver. The show elicited letters to the station from all around the region. It was still not enough to convince the station to go with it. They thought a one-half hour show might work better. By this time, both Nan and I were thinking that maybe our problem was we were thinking too small. Just maybe, we needed to be thinking of a national show instead of a local Denver show. That idea began to germinate.

While all of this was going on, something else was happening that seemed trivial at the time, but deserves mention now. Margaret's boss had come to her and said, Equifax has credit reports we are doing for customers in Denver. Currently, we are having to mail them which delays the process by several days. It seems like Rex is going to Denver nearly every day. Do you think he would be interested in delivering those credit reports for us and they would get there the same day? Margaret told her she didn't think I would be interested, but she would ask. When she told me about it, I said, we need the extra money, I would be glad to do it. I began delivering credit reports in Denver as a part of my trip. The customers they had took only about one to two hours and still gave me time to do what I was doing on "Little Stars".

The idea of a national show had now gone full circle. We had studied the market, learned how shows were syndicated and had decided what was needed was a completed show that would be the vehicle for syndication. To do this required more money. Most syndicated shows are owned by individual investors. A half hour show that may air over and over again for years can produce a great deal of income. I had already set up a new corporation, International Media Productions. Under that umbrella, I was able to sell half hour shows on spec. The investors, which were mainly people I knew personally, were told what we were doing was highly speculative, and I could give no guarantees of success; but, if we could pull it off, it could be a big win for them. What they were buying was only a partial interest in a half hour show. We retained a portion. Each half hour was $10,000.00. There were no investors that could not afford to lose their investment. They bought in because they believed the project was a worthwhile one and they believed it would work.

Our pilot program was to be filmed at a studio in Hollywood. Nan hired her original director for "Little Stars" in Chicago. He flew to Hollywood for the filming. Nan and I had gone to Hollywood two weeks early to audition talent and we used two of the best acts from our Denver show. The format called for each show to feature a big star that had once been a "Little Star". For the first show we selected Margaret O'Brian. She had won an Oscar for "Meet Me in St. Louis" and had many other famous roles. She was hired for just the one show. In an interesting aside, after that one appearance, she applied for unemployment and my corporation was informed that we would be responsible for a portion of her unemployment. Live and learn.

The day of the taping was an exciting one. The studio had three separate studios so three things could be taped at the same time. That day, one studio had a crew making a commercial with a popular female icon billed as "the cucaracha girl" .The second studio was doing a promo for the Dick Van Patten show. We were in studio three. When it came time for lunch break, Dick Van Patten was gracious enough to lend us his limousine and driver. We took the kids on the show to the Brown Derby for lunch. The one thing I remember about that lunch was one of the kids spotted Roddy McDowall sitting at one of the tables studying a script. The youngster boldly went over to the table and asked for an autograph. He was rather rudely rebuffed. My opinion of Roddy McDowell went way down. However, in the interest of fairness, I should point out that it must be difficult for stars to deal with a fawning public. You can't even have a peaceful meal. Still, I would have signed the autograph.

With the pilot in the can, I set about marketing it nationally. I made appointments with each of the major networks and then flew to New York. It was familiar territory when I stepped into the elevator to go to NBC. It was the same elevator that I had used for Amy Lorton McKay. I checked where her office had been. It was no longer there. One by one, I made my pitch to each network and their production people. Each one was shown the pilot and format for future shows. With each network, I began to hear the same mantra. A talent show was fine back in the days of "Major Bowes", but today's audiences are too sophisticated to have a great interest in a talent show. It became obvious that this was not going to work. The only option would be to syndicate the show, and then sell it to television stations individually. I needed a syndicator. Still in New York, I began calling on syndicators. When I reached Allworld Telefilm Sales Corporation and their president, Gustave Nathan, I found a believer. He was the syndicator for "Bozo the Clown" and about ten other shows including the "Playboy Show" and the "Playmate of the Year Special". He said that he had long believed that the market might be right for a talent show, especially one that featured kids. He had been closely associated with the people surrounding the old "Major Bowes" show. Mr. Nathan became our syndicator.

The way it works in the syndication world is a convention is held once a year by the NAIT, the National Association of Independent Television Producers and Distributors, where every television station in the country comes to purchase their programming for the next year. All of the syndicated shows have their booth set up and their wares on display. The ones like Gustave Nathan, who had multiple shows, had a suite set up with food and drink and all the bells and whistles. Of course, syndicators made calls individually on stations throughout the year but, this convention was the main vehicle for sales. The convention that year was being held in San Francisco. I took my entire family to the convention along with Nan. The first day it was raining and I had some difficulty getting a valet to get the rental car parked. When I walked into the lobby of the convention center, Margaret was holding an elevator for me. Apparently, she had been holding it for a good minute or so, and there were three other people on the elevator with her and my children. They turned out to be Chuck Connors and two girls with him, one draped on each arm. He was at the convention with his "Rifleman" show. When I got on the elevator, I was damp from the rain and my hair was disheveled. Mr. Connors was obviously a bit hung over, and annoyed for having to wait a minute. He made a rather disparaging remark about my appearance and the girls gave him a supportive giggle. I don't remember my comeback, but I know my children's opinion of Mr. Connors would never be the same.

My boys were all agog in our suite we were sharing with Bozo the clown, and the Playboy Playmate of the Year. They were even more wide eyed when the Playmate of the Year asked them to escort her through the convention to visit all the booths. It gave her a safe escort and two eager boys were more than glad to oblige. Even though the convention turned out to be pretty much a bust for our show, my family had a great time. They met a host of stars in the various booths and suites. Tony and Drew were especially thrilled to meet and shake hands with John Wayne's son, Pat. His suite was bustling with lots of good food. It was an exciting week for the family with dinner in Chinatown, and visits to the San Francisco sights.

I said the convention turned out to be a bust for the show. Almost everyone liked the pilot, but, there was concern for the fact we only had one show in the can. Even though we had a good plan in place for the rapid production of the entire series, they were reluctant to commit the time on their stations without the certainty of at least 16 weeks in advance. That is really understandable when you know how station scheduling is done. Many had the same criticism that we had heard from the networks. A talent show was fine in "Major Bowes" era, but we don't think it would play well for today's audiences. One of the companies that gave us the most attention was Bob Banner Productions. They had a number of syndicated shows of their own. Over the next several months we continued to search for other answers. We attended one more convention in Las Vegas; but, in the end, we decided we did not have sufficient funding to proceed and the entire project was discontinued.

In a postscript to this story, Bob Banner Productions, who had shown a great deal of interest in both "Little Stars" and our plans for "Your Big Break" apparently combined our formats. They hired Ed McMahon and produced the first three episodes of "Star Search". After that it was picked up by the network. The audiences that the networks said were too sophisticated for a talent show have over the last thirty plus years seen "Star Search", "America's Got Talent, "The Voice", and a number of other amateur talent shows become audience favorites. We were just a little ahead of our time and perhaps made some mistakes in marketing.

11

Remember You Are an Entreprenuer

DURING THE TIME I HAD BEEN ABSENT, I ARRANGED FOR my son to take the Equifax credit reports to Denver. When I got back to take care of it myself, I discovered that a number of the Equifax customers in Colorado Springs had learned that we were delivering credit reports to Denver, and they wondered if we would be interested in doing some deliveries and pick-ups for them. At that time, every mortgage company had files going regularly to VA and FHA and files coming back. In a matter of several weeks, I had signed up over ten companies that wanted service to Denver with round trips to both VA and FHA. This was the beginning of a brand new business. I set up Sample Couriers and began to build. There is an old saying, if you want a successful business, find a need and fill it. I hadn't been looking for this one. It found me. But, I was at least wise enough to sense an opportunity and grab hold of it.

Over the next year my business grew quickly. I was surprised that someone had not already taped into this market. I needed to acquire a PUC license, which I did, and get business insurance on vehicles that were used for delivery. When the deliveries became too much for me, I hired my son. When it became too much for two of us, I hired Drew's new wife. By the end of the first year, I had six full time drivers. Each driver was an independent contractor working on a percentage. They had to provide their own vehicle and insurance and follow all the rules of our little operation. We almost called the company Executive Couriers because we wanted to put forth the image of being a company that would go beyond the normal requirements of a delivery service. We didn't take that name, but we did successfully engender that image.

Within two years, we had found a host of new markets. We were now delivering credit reports for, not just Equifax but all of the credit reporting agencies. We had signed contracts with most of the mortgage companies in Colorado Springs and had also signed up a number of banks that needed service to Denver. Many of the Denver companies had signed with us as well and we had expanded to include Fort Collins, Loveland, and Boulder as well as Pueblo and Canon City. By the end of our third year we had sixteen full time drivers. Over the next twenty years, Sample Couriers became the "get well" solution for my entire family. Whenever one of them was out of work, we became their temporary solution. During that time my drivers included both my sons, my daughter Alexis and her husband, both my sons' wives, three of my brothers and two of their wives, a grandson, and did I forget, Margaret ran a route also. What had started out as just a courtesy for Margaret's boss had turned into the most successful business I had created.

One of my largest customers had become Mortgage Guarantee Insurance Corporation. They wrote Mortgage Insurance for any loan but primarily on FHA loans. They had paper work going back and forth to all the mortgage companies and we carried it all. We had set up an office in Denver out near the Bronco stadium. The couriers came there for their lunch break and to exchange packages going from north to south. Our northern couriers lived in or around Loveland so they could be close to home when they finished their days run. The ones covering Pueblo and Canon City lived in Colorado Springs. The Denver couriers lived in Denver. When our work for MGIC proved very successful, the Vice President called me into his office. He said, we need the same service you are providing us here for El Paso and Albuquerque. Do you think you would be interested in doing it? They were the controlling office for the entire region. What they wanted was someone to go to all the companies they serviced in those cities and pick up the insurance apps and then send them by overnight express to Denver. Then someone had to pick them up and deliver them to MGIC. Each day the approvals would then be expressed back and delivered in each market. That service would cut two days off their time of service. I told him, if I can make it work, I will.

Over the next two months, I found someone else to run my route in Denver and flew to Albuquerque first and set up an office and hired couriers. Before I left I was able to sign up enough of the same customers we had in Colorado in the New Mexico market to make it profitable for the couriers. When I had Albuquerque up and running, I flew to El Paso and did the same thing. Within four months Sample Couriers was a factor in three states. It now became necessary for me to make regular trips to oversee what was happening in each market and to sell more customers to expand the market and make it more profitable.

On one of my trips to Albuquerque, I received a call from the Vice President of MGIC. He was in town and wanted to see me. I met him at the Ambassador Inn. He had been calling on their customers in town, and he just wanted me to know how pleased they were with our service. He and I had visited on a number of occasions and had discovered we had a lot in common. We genuinely liked each other and it was obvious he just wanted my company and wanted to have a chance to visit. The nation was just entering a period of crisis with the crash of the stock market and the real estate market was beginning to take a big hit. While we were at the table visiting, he received a telephone call. When he got off the phone he said, MGIC just received its first claim. They had been in business for years, but they had never had a claim till now.

I didn't say anything, but I was flabbergasted. All those years they had pure profit with no claims. The next five years made up for that.

Each year we had been having one day set aside as an appreciation day to all the couriers. They brought their families for a full day of food and fun. At some point, we decided that this needed to be an appreciation day for our entire customer base. The first one was held at Lakeside Amusement Park in Denver. All of the mortgage companies from up and down the front ridge that were our customers, the banks, the savings and loans, everyone we serviced were invited to a full day of food and fun. They brought their families. The children were each given passes to the rides. At the end of the day, the children went home. Some of the parents came back for the dance. We had rented a dance pavilion. Our country western band provided the music. I had supplemented it with Archie Davis, one of the great fiddle players from Nashville and a steel guitar man that was a personal friend of Chet Atkins and had recorded with him. Most of my family participated. Alexis, with her Patsy Cline type voice, did several numbers as did both of my sons. I played guitar and acted as host and front man. The event proved to be a great success. It had been expensive, but it paid dividends in business. From that time, it became an annual event. One year it was at Elitch Gardens, one year it was at a rented American Legion Hall, one year it was at Flying W Ranch in the Garden of the Gods. All great memories.

We have been talking about all of the good things from those years, but we need to look at some of the bad and the ugly, as well. One day while on the route, I was heading toward downtown Denver on a one way street. The traffic was moving quite rapidly. I was in the left hand lane when suddenly a car came bursting into the intersection from a cross street and went directly in front of me. There was not even time to try to hit a brake. I hit the car broadside and sent it flying. I had my seat belt on or I would have died that day. As it was, I was badly hurt. All I remember, is someone asking, is he dead? Someone else said, we don't know yet. They transported me to Denver General's ER. In the emergency room, I was able to talk and communicate. They feared internal injuries and bleeding and needed to use a belly probe with a camera to find out but, they were afraid to use an anesthesia. I can tell you that is not a pleasant way to spend an afternoon. Fortunately, my injuries were mostly superficial except for the whiplash which remains a problem even today. The young lady I hit survived as well. She had just learned her brother had been killed in the Iran-Iraq war. She was a foreign national living in the United States. She had no insurance on the car and she had no license to drive. She was crying as she drove and just went into the intersection blind. My guardian Angel was with me that day.

Both of my sons enlisted in the Air Force right out of high school. I had dreamed of them going on to college and following in my footsteps, but each of us must make our own decisions and we can't live their life for them. That is a reality that every parent has a problem resolving. We must each make our own mistakes, or what might seem a mistake to us at the time. Drew wanted to work with dogs, so he became part of the canine unit. Tony became an avionics specialist and served in Germany. From there, he flew to Spain and Italy and Greece to service the fleet. While there, he met a girl who was in avionics with him. They were married by the time they returned to the states and ended their enlistment. When they got back, they both needed employment, so Sample Couriers became their first job back. They both worked for me for two years. The rest of this story is hard to relate.

Tony and Nora were living in Aurora. They had just hosted a party for the family where we took our instruments and recorded a bunch of music with the family all performing. Later that night, Tony had a Grand Mal seizure which would not abate. He was rushed to the VA hospital in Denver because they had no insurance and Sample Couriers did not provide insurance. At the VA we learned Tony was suffering from brain cancer and would require surgery. His cancer was a type that wraps itself around the brain stem like gelatin. There was no assurance that surgery could be successful. The VA Hospital was just across the street from Colorado General which was the best in Denver. They worked with the VA. A brilliant surgeon from there performed the surgery. He told us bluntly that what he had done was only going to give Tony a few more years. He was unable to get it all without destroying his brain stem which would have made him a vegetable.

What had happened to Tony shook me to my core. There was a great sense of guilt that we had not provided Tony insurance. That one event led to what, in retrospect, I believe was a bad business decision. I decided that Sample Couriers needed to change its policy. Up till now, all the couriers had been independent contractors. From now on, they would be employees. We would deduct social security and taxes and provide an insurance package for the entire family. In addition to added cost to the company, it meant a lot more work and cost in dealing with payroll and all of the government requirements. I would come to regret having made that choice.

When Tony recovered from his surgery, he and Nora decided to move to California. Nan had gone to California where Judy lived in Gilroy. Once there, she had opened a flower and gift shop and was doing well. She believed she could provide Nora with employment and Tony wanted to start college. That area also put him close to Stanford Medical Center for his continued cancer monitoring. Much of the next few years is rather a blur for me. Tony survived long enough to father three grandchildren, and complete two years of college. When his cancer again became critical, a second surgery was performed at Stanford Medical Center in Palo Alto. From there, he went directly to a VA nursing home in San Jose where he would spend the remainder of his life. When I received the call that Tony was becoming critical, I flew to San Jose. Alexis was already living in California with Nora. She had wanted to be closer to Tony. She and Tony had always had a very close relationship. When I arrived at the nursing home to see Tony, the doctor took me aside and told me Tony only had few days to live. I spent the next day struggling with myself. It was payroll time in Colorado. I had couriers that were depending on me for their livelihood. I made the decision that I needed to go home. I went in to see Tony one last time and had a prayer with him. I knew I would never see him again. I left the room and went into the hallway where I broke down and began to cry. One of the doctors came up to see if I was alright and I explained what was happening. He put his arm around me and led me out of the building. The responsibility now fell on Alexis to be there when he died. She was with him. It would be years before she would forgive me for not having been there too. We had two memorial services for Tony. One in California where he was put to rest at Golden Gate National Cemetery just north of San Francisco. The second service in Colorado for all the family and friends there. Over the years, I conducted funeral services for my mother, my sister Dorothy, my oldest brother, my brother's wife, as well as dozens of parishioners; and now, Tony. It was the hardest service I had ever conducted.

It was now necessary to work even harder to keep the business healthy. My decision to make all the couriers employee's had cut the profit margin and made us a little less competitive. A number of competitors had come into the market. Trip Savers in Colorado Springs and three primary competitors in Denver. My answer was to find additional ways to either enlarge our customer base or develop new markets. We looked at the possibility of expanding into a national company. All of the cost studies on the revenue required for such a move made it unfeasible. Then we looked at the possibility of going after just California. A study of California regulations sent chills up my back. That idea was discarded. I remembered that when I was attending the race track regularly, many of the gamblers had difficulty getting to the track. The way Colorado operated its greyhound tracks, the season would start with a three month run in Loveland. Then it would move to Denver and Pueblo. They would run simultaneously. Then the Colorado Springs track would run for three months. In the winter, the greyhounds would move to the Interstate Track which was located about fifty miles east of Denver. It was basically a twelve month schedule. Meanwhile, there was Centennial Race Track that ran horses all summer in the afternoon. I knew there was a large pool of gamblers living in the Colorado Springs area that went to all those meets regularly. It looked to me like an opportunity.

I went to the PUC and acquired a license for carrying passengers, purchased an eighteen passenger van, and announced service to all of the tracks. For a while, I drove the van myself. From the first day, we were full. The charge was reasonable, certainly less than the gas and wear and tear on their automobiles. We arranged for a program seller located right next door to the bus station to take reservation calls for the van. We did the pick up at his location. It was good extra business for him and very convenient for us. Plus, the tracks had all given me a bonus by giving each of my riders free programs and free admission. When the gamblers got out of the track they were always hungry. My daughter, Terri, found herself with a little business of her own. Each day she would make sandwiches which were stored in the vans cold box. In addition to sandwiches she had candy bars and soft drinks. Nearly every day we would sell out all the food. Quite often, the gamblers would be broke when the races were over. We always gave them credit. Gamblers are the most honorable people with their debt. In all the time we ran the van, I never had one welcher. I say it was Terri's concession; in fairness, I have to tell you that Margaret was the enabler, but she wanted Terri to have the credit. When the van was running smoothly, I hired a driver. We ran the van to the horse track for the afternoon program, then to the dog track at night. Many of the riders would be the same for both trips. Centennial track actually started naming one of their feature stakes races after our bus, The Sample Courier Stakes. Can you believe it? Burning the candle at both ends, working during the day and driving the van at night was becoming too much and, I still needed to cover Albuquerque and El Paso.

It was on one of my trips to El Paso that another ugly reality found me. I had a severe angina attach. When I got back to Denver the doctors performed an emergency angiogram followed by angioplasty. My main artery was over 95% blocked. Rather than to repeat stories on this issue, I will simply tell you that over the next few years, angioplasty was required twice more and then it was followed by open heart surgery with a six-way by pass. It was clear that I needed to slow down a little bit.

Sometimes slowing down is easier said than done. Another opportunity presented itself. We had been doing some courier work for one of the local mortuaries. One day, the owner said we have a need if you would be interested in filling it. We need someone who can transport bodies to locales that do not have air service available. We have people who come to Colorado Springs for treatment, die here, and then wish to be interred in their home town. We have been having to use our drivers, but that is running us too thin. Also, we have bodies that need to go to Denver that have been donated for medical research and for the harvesting of body parts. We are certainly not the only ones in town that have need of this service. To make a rather long story short, I ended up purchasing a Grand Caravan and had a slider installed in the back in order to transport caskets. I, also, bought a hearse. We began transporting bodies both in and out of state. I set up a separate operation for this and Drew managed it. We used the hearse for short hauls and the Grand Caravan for the long ones. The hearse was also available for mortuaries to rent, along with our driver, when they needed an extra hearse.

During those years, Margaret had her challenges, as well. Early on in our marriage she had required surgery to remove her thyroid. Now, she was diagnosed with breast cancer. They gave her an option of removal of just the immediately affected part to be followed by radiation and chemotherapy or to undergo a total mastectomy. She opted for the later. Over the years the residual nerves have continued to bother her but, I think, she still feels she made the right decision as there has been no reoccurrence.

Over this twenty year period of time, Sample Couriers continued to be the primary vehicle that sustained our immediate family and many in our extended family. But, now, three things were about to happen that was going to change all of that. The first, and most damaging was the advent of the INTERNET. Almost overnight, customers began cancelling as they were able to transmit credit reports over the internet and cut two days off their time of service. This eliminated most of the credit agencies. MGIC could now transmit all of their insurance apps and return approvals over the internet. Albuquerque and El Paso became the first victims. Without MGIC and the credit companies, the residual business was not enough to sustain an office. Both closed.

The second shoe dropped when the State of Colorado discovered that the mortuary in Colorado Springs that had been our primary customer had been guilty of a number of serious violations of State Law including embezzlement. They came in and locked the door. Without their business, I decided the profit margin would be too low to justify continuance. We sold the hearse and van and said goodbye to the funeral business. The third shoe dropped when the State of Colorado decided to close all the greyhound tracks by not granting them another license. Centennial Race Track had also closed. They were in process of building a new track east of town, but for now, that was no longer a business. We sold the passenger van.

Even with all of those things gone, Sample Couriers was still viable. We had enough other business to sustain it, but with just a few couriers. It continued to be our needed source of income. During all this time, I had continued my relationship with the church. Sunday's would find me teaching my adult Bible Study at Calvary United Methodist Church. When the pastor would have to be absent for Annual Conference or some other engagement, he would ask me to fill the pulpit. In June of 2007, the pastor had

Annual Conference. Again he asked me to fill the pulpit. The next week when I entered my classroom for Bible Study, two in my class spoke up and said, Rex, we really enjoyed your service last week and we think you should consider going back where you belong. You need to be in full time Christian service. I was a bit surprised and taken a little off guard. I said, who would want a 76 year old ex preacher? Their response was, how do you know unless you try?

I had truthfully never considered that possibility. I thought there was too much history, and all of that was in my past; but, the confidence of my class and the prayer they offered up on my behalf, caused a stirring in my soul. Maybe they were right. The first thing I did was to gather my family around and ask their opinion. Did they think it would be something I should consider? The vote was unanimous. Drew said, I will help you get your resume together and get it on the internet for you. The others were equally helpful. In just over three days, we had a resume on the internet. Just a few days later, we had a response from a church in Liberia. They had an opening for an English speaking pastor and they would be willing to make me an offer. Margaret said, if you are going to Liberia, you will have to go alone. A short time later, we had a call from Munds Park, Arizona. That story is coming next.

12

Returning to My Hearts Desire

IT WAS ONLY A FEW DAYS BEFORE THERE WAS A CALL from the Chairman of the Search Committee for Munds Park Community Church in Munds Park, Arizona, requesting a personal interview. For this part of the story, I am relying on the information given to me by one of the committee members, Lynn Rouyer. According to Lynn, after initially reviewing my resume it had been placed in the reject pile. Somehow it found its way back into the might consider pile. Then, it somehow found its way back into the pile of candidates to be interviewed. No one seems to know how that happened. Margaret and I traveled to Munds Park for the interview. They had apparently interviewed several ahead of me. One of the first questions that was put to me by the committee was, if we were to select you, what would be your financial requirement? Where the church is concerned, money had never been a part of my consideration, even during the hard times. My answer was simple. Whatever the Board of Elders decides is fair, that will be acceptable to me. It would be my pleasure to serve.

That first interview resulted in an offer to return for a Sunday service which we did. The congregation voted and we were overwhelmingly accepted. In the fall of 2007, with several dozen candidates being considered, I had been returned to my heart's desire. Remarkable! My acceptance, while it was exciting to ponder this new opportunity to serve, caught me a bit off guard. I think I really didn't expect it to happen. I still owned Sample Couriers. There were still routes to run and work to be done. A date had now been set for me to begin. There was much to do.

There was a company in town that specialized in selling businesses, but their average time for accomplishing that was still several months, and they charged an arm and a leg for their service. My closest competitor in Colorado Springs had been Trip Savers. The owner and I had visited on a number of occasions. I knew that he had long coveted my customer base. One call to test the waters found a more than receptive response. We met in his office. In the course of one afternoon we had a signed agreement. I had no hard assets to sell, only an established customer base that was still producing a good monthly gross, and several good, dedicated couriers that had been with me for a long time. I had told him that I was going to return to where I began, serving the Lord. He was a Christian man and a leader in his church. He understood. I, also, told him that any sale had to include an accommodation for all of my couriers. To this, he readily agreed. I prepared a letter to all of my customers thanking them for their years of loyalty to Sample Couriers and assuring them that there would be no change in their service. After nearly thirty years, Sample Couriers was history. On a trip to Colorado several years later, I went to see one of my original couriers, Bob Gates. Bob was still running a small route at the age of 91. The group of banks he serviced loved him and Trip Savers had faithfully kept him on. I was gratified.

With my affairs in Colorado Springs in order, all that was left was to pack up and move. Margaret's brother, Norman, agreed to come along and drive the van with our furniture. We followed with the car. We had already located a home in Munds Park for rent. Norman helped us move in before flying back to Colorado.

That first week in Munds Park was one of learning. I discovered to my delight that Munds Park Community Church had no debt. In fact, because of generous benefactors they had substantial reserves. Most churches have to deal with either looming debt, or conference obligations that stretch their budget. This church had neither. No pastor likes to feel he must hound his congregation for money. We are called upon to honor the tithe, but beyond that, we are reluctant to go. This would make it possible for me to concentrate on the more important elements of ministry.

I soon discovered that the church did face some significant challenges. Munds Park was a divided community. As the only established church in town, I felt it was incumbent on us to try to turn that around. There were open sores between the church and the Catholic community. There were several factions is town that resented the church and would have liked nothing better than to see it go away. There were some strong divisions within the business community and, as is typical in these situations, everyone believes that they are right. Where to begin?

One of the first efforts was to try to bring the Catholic and Protestant community together. The Catholics had previously requested permission to use the church for their services on Saturday. That request had been denied by the church board. I challenged the board to change their mind pointing out that we all worship the same God and even though our belief system is different, we have an obligation to accommodate each other. It took some doing, but the board agreed and the Catholics began holding services on Saturday in the church. The result was a rapid easing of tensions between the two groups. We were starting to come together.

I believed it was important that the influence of the church be felt across the community. To do this, I made a point of joining almost every community organization in town. This resulted in my being asked to be Chaplain for the Pinewood Fire Department. That was a duty I gladly performed for the entirety of my time in

Munds Park. When I became a limited member of the Pinewood Country Club, I noticed a gradual change in some of the attitudes from that group of elites, some of whom felt that they were just a cut above the rest of the community. Quite a few from the country club became my friends and some even joined the church.

I discovered the same frosty reception when I first visited the RV Park and Resort that was just east of the church. I had gone there to put up a poster on their bulletin board announcing the time of various services at the church. I was refused permission to put up my poster. There was still much work to be done. It had always been my belief that the church should be the focal point for any healthy community. It could certainly be claimed that this was one of the great American traditions in thousands of little towns across America. The church was the primary focal point. This was where you came to marry and to bury. It was the Alpha and the Omega. It hosted community meetings as well as church meetings. It was my wish to accomplish that in Munds Park. The community was made aware that the church was open and available to any legitimate group or organization.

In my very first year, we learned that Munds Park can be a dangerous place in the winter time. The worst blizzard in many years hit northern Arizona. My house was nearly covered. There was just a crack to see out the front window. Dozens of motorists were stranded on I-17. The community of Munds Park jumped into action. The church was the only logical place for a shelter. Highway patrol and the fire department began bringing the stranded into the church. The ladies from the Fire Auxiliary prepared food. For two days, the church was the only game in town. One of the local eateries had used a snow mobile to deliver food to stranded motorists that couldn't make it to the church. Late in the second day, a reporter and camera man from Fox News in Phoenix somehow found their way to Munds Park. The resulting pictures and interviews made their way onto the evening news and then was picked up by the national news media. Munds Park was on the national news.

Among the stranded travelers were people from all over the world. There was a group of soldiers from Iraq that were in the United States for flight training by the US military. There was a couple from England and one couple from Australia. On the second day, we held a special church service to celebrate the deliverance of all these folks from the ravages of the blizzard. Everyone attended and with the volunteers and the firemen and some of the locals, the church was nearly full. The letters the church received back from these grateful travelers should remain as cherished memories.

It became obvious that the church was the most convenient and likely spot to establish a shelter to meet this type of crisis. A call to Red Cross headquarters confirmed their interest in having such a shelter in Munds Park. However, to be a recognized Red Cross shelter and receive Red Cross support required that you have back-up power. In other words, your own generator. The experience we had just had with the blizzard had caused a coalescence within the community. They had done something important. Important enough to make the national news. Everyone felt good about themselves. The Munds Park Home Owners Association, a group that had also been a bit stand offish, stepped forward and financed a new generator for the church. The ladies of the Fire Auxiliary purchased a freezer and stocked it with food. The Red Cross brought in 50 cots and stored them in our storage facility. The entire community had come together to make that possible. I sensed that what I had hoped for was beginning to happen.

In my third year, I was approached by one of my new members, Bill Spain, who was at that time the second largest realtor in town. He, and his wife, had converted from the Catholic faith to become members of Munds Park Community Church. He believed that the community badly needed a strong business alliance that could enforce some standards of conduct for the entire local business establishment. The feeling was that there had been some rather unethical practices in the past and that needed to stop. I supported him in his efforts, but it was largely because of his tenacity and dedication to service that the Munds Park Business Alliance was formed. They met regularly at the church and within a year ii included most of the businesses in town. They became a strong voice for ethical business practices and a leader in a variety of community projects including beautification projects, tree planting, and signage off the highway. Another milestone in bringing the community together.

One of the most important elements in bringing the community together occurred when two rather determined and dedicated ladies requested permission to start a Farmers Market on the front parking lot of the church. The market would be on Saturday's and they assured us they had venders available from the markets they were running in Phoenix and some of our own members could benefit by having such a market. Farmer's Markets were no stranger to me. We had used them in New York and Nebraska. They were always popular and a good thing for the community. After setting some standards that would have to be met, the board agreed, and the Farmers Market became a reality. It was successful from the start. The church had its own booth. Most Saturdays, I manned the booth myself with a couple of volunteers. It gave us an opportunity to reach out to visitors and invite them to church as well as promote the church agenda. Dozens of visitors to Munds Park sent back letters remarking about the great experience that they had here and saying they had enjoyed our church service. It was a good thing.

When I had been in Shandaken, New York, I had the feeling that I would be happy to spend the rest of my life there. I had that same feeling about Walsh, Colorado and, now, I had that same feeling about Munds Park, Arizona. Life is never really about how much stuff we have or even how much money we have in the bank. It's about having a purpose that is important and having the internal peace that comes with knowing you are fulfilling that purpose. Over the years, I had served God in a myriad of ways both in and out of the church. Even when I was not serving as a full time pastor, the opportunities to serve God always presented themselves whether it was driving a Yellow Cab, or speaking to senators. Now, after spending the majority of my life doing secular work, I was being rewarded by being able to return to my heart's desire. God is, indeed, good.

There is no need to relate a blow by blow account of all that happened in my five years in Munds Park. That would be too lengthy and somewhat redundant. For the most part, it was a rewarding and deeply gratifying experience. During that time, Margaret and I celebrated our fiftieth wedding anniversary by going to Maui. I had long promised her a trip to Hawaii. This one was made possible by the generosity of one of our members who had a condo in Maui that he graciously allowed us to use. It was an unforgettable trip. I had the opportunity to do some of the things that brought personal satisfaction like playing the role of the gambler in the Pinewood Players production of "Guys and Dolls". I was secretly amused by thinking they were type casting. It was great fun.

Entering my sixth year, a disagreement arose on the church board. They voted to discontinue the Farmer's Market. The argument had been about having the market on Saturday which some thought made it difficult to have church functions on that day. That argument was really a straw dog. The reality was there was no church function that could not be managed even with the market. The real reason was a theological one. There was a group who believed having the Farmers Market on church property somehow violated the moral imperatives of the church. The reference was to the incident recorded in the Gospels where Jesus ran the money changers out of the Temple in Jerusalem. I had pointed out on several occasions that the objection Jesus had was not an objection to the market. The market had been on Temple grounds for centuries. It was the place all of Jerusalem came to purchase produce and goods. The objection Jesus had was the fact that the Temple had created its own coinage. They had decreed that anything purchased from the market had to be purchased with Temple coinage. That meant exchanging your Roman, or

Greek, or Turkish coins for Temple coins. To do that required paying an exchange fee that amounted to usury. Jesus saw this practice as abominable. The entire system had become corrupt. When families brought their own animals for sacrifice, they were told they were unacceptable. It had to be Temple livestock. The Temple would then buy the livestock from the family and sell them Temple livestock. The Temple would then turn around and sell the same livestock back to the next family as having been purified. I believe a strong case can be made that Jesus objected, not only to that practice, but also the practice of animal sacrifice. The Gospel of John places this event at the early part of Jesus ministry. John is the only one that uses the word "market" in the critic of Jesus. The other three Gospel writers all place this event at the end of Jesus ministry just before his crucifixion. They all three, emphasize the critic of Jesus being about the money changers and the practice of buying and selling animals for sacrifice. He said, "My house is a house of worship. You have turned it into a den of thieves". With that he used a whip made of cords to drive the money changers out of the Temple and overturned their tables. This was one of his final acts of disobedience before his crucifixion. We know that Jesus saw his sacrifice as the ultimate sacrifice for all of mankind for the atonement of sin. If he also saw it as an end to all animal sacrifice, that did not happen. The practice continued in the Temple until 70 AD when Roman soldiers sacked Jerusalem and completely destroyed the Temple. The Temple grounds had been the size of 15 football fields. That was where all of the animal sacrifices took place. When the Temple was rebuilt it did not have the large Temple grounds and the practice was discontinued. It continued, however, in individual Jewish homes until late in the Second Century.

The nearly unanimous vote of the board to close the market despite my strong objection, led me to believe I no longer had the moral authority to lead this congregation. I chose to retire. We had already purchased a retirement home in Camp Verde, and I was eighty one years old. It was time to turn over the reins to someone younger and more vigorous. In November of 2013, I gave my farewell sermon. What began with a sermon to a Presbyterian congregation in Sidney, Nebraska at the age of 16 had ended with a sermon to a beloved congregation in Munds Park, Arizona, at the age of 81. Had I chosen to take my issue on the market to a congregational vote, I have little doubt, I would have prevailed; but, it was my feeling that this would only tend to divide a community I had spent the last five years trying to bring together. I still believe I made the right choice. In a postscript to the story, the market has, since my retirement, been restored and is thriving as we speak, and Margaret and I have been honored to be remembered by the church for our efforts while there. A property directly behind the church that I had attempted to acquire has since been purchased by the church, and my efforts had helped make that possible.

Since our retirement, Margaret and I have lived peacefully enjoying our final years. This, despite a number of health challenges that are just a part of growing older. We continue to see a number of our former congregants and their continued love and support have made our retirement easier. One of them even took us on a weekend trip to a Wyndham Resort in San Diego. Through it all, God has been our constant companion. In my final two chapters we will be talking about that in detail. Those final two chapters are the reason for writing this autobiography. Hopefully, you will find something that will help you in your search for the Father.

13

A Retrospective on Divine Providence

IT IS MY BELIEF THAT MY LIFE HAS BEEN DIRECTLY influenced over the years by Divine Providence. In this next chapter, I will attempt to make that case. However, to do so, will require a good deal of preparation on the part of my readers. I will break this chapter down into sections. This will enable me to delineate my faith and will help my reader understand it. This chapter may be a difficult one for my Evangelical friends to stomach. If that proves to be true, I apologize in advance but, I must in good conscience, tell it like I see it.

THE SCHISM BETWEEN SCIENCE AND THE COMMUNITY OF FAITH

The conflict between science and the faith community has been going on for centuries. It is my contention that it need not be so. There is much that the faith community can contribute to the unanswered questions of science, and the science community can be an enormous help to the faith community if allowed to do so. Let me point out in the beginning that neither side in this argument is without blemish. History has demonstrated many cases where the faith community was flat wrong. That same thing can be said of the science community. Let me give you a couple of examples. The church for many years maintained that the earth was flat. Anyone who disagreed with that position was charged with apostasy and was severely punished. Science had already declared that the earth was round. It was not until Columbus sailed in 1492 and did not fall off the end of the earth that the church was forced to acknowledge their error. Perhaps the best example I can give you on the imperfections in science is the one that is playing out right now as we speak. There is a large body of scientists that are convinced beyond any doubt that climate change and global warming are the result of man generated greenhouse gases. It is their contention that if we do not curb carbon emissions drastically in the next few years, our planet is in severe danger. There is an equally large number of respected and highly capable climatologists who disagree. They contend that while they acknowledge that there are some changes taking place in the climate that those changes are a part of the normal weather cycle that has been going on for centuries. They say that carbon emissions account for only a very tiny percentage of climate change. Hardly enough to measure. It goes without saying, both positions cannot be true. One or the other is wrong.

There have been many other examples of this ongoing battle over the years. In the past two hundred years, perhaps none more notable than the John Scopes trial in 1925. John Scopes had been accused of teaching evolution in his Arkansas classroom. Because of the sensitivity of the issue at the time, the trial garnered national attention. William Jennings Bryan, from Nebraska was chosen to lead the prosecution. Bryan had three times run for President and had been soundly defeated all three times, but he was a well-known public figure and noted for his oratory and grandiose presentations of biblical truth. Clarence Darrow, a brilliant lawyer from Chicago was recruited for the defense. Darrow was the son of a minister, but he had become an agnostic. This whole story is told in Hollywood fashion in the movie "Inherit the Wind" starring Spencer Tracy as Clarence Darrow and Frederic March as Bryan. In the course of the trial, Darrow succeeds in getting Bryan to take the stand. When he does, he begins to ask him questions about the Bible. Bryan contends that the Bible is correct in every detail right down to each period and comma. It is the revealed word of God and is to be accepted exactly as it is. Darrow proceeds to take Bryan apart. The history is that John Scopes was still found guilty even though Darrow had out shown Bryan in the trial.

A little known postscript to this story is worth mentioning. After the Scopes trial, Darrow had made some public pronouncements that had infuriated the faith community. Bishop McConnell of the Methodist Church rose to the occasion and challenged Darrow to a debate on the existence of God. Darrow was still full of himself from the Scopes trial. He gladly accepted. The result was predictable. Darrow was in way over his head. Bishop McConnell literally tore him to shreds. It would be years before Darrow fully recovered his reputation. He went on to make a name for himself in civil liberty cases.

No place is this schism between science and faith more apparent than in reconciling the work of science and the community of faith as regards the Bible. The faith community still clings to the conviction that the Biblical story of creation is literally true. In seven days God created everything that exists with man being his final creation. Let us look for a minute at what science has been able to tell us. Since the time of Hubbell and the advent of deep space probes we have discovered that the universe is far more expansive than anyone knew or even guessed. Not only that, we have learned that it is expanding rapidly with new galaxies being added at a rapid pace. Because of this new knowledge, science has been able to determine the age of the universe. It is now calculated that the universe began 10 to 15 billion years ago. There is evidence to support that it began abruptly. This has given rise to the "Big Bang" theory. From a single atom exploding with the energy within it to create a universe. Even if that is what happened, it does not answer the question of where did that atom come from and who or what was responsible for its explosion. God still has to be part of that equation.

Science has, also, been able to date the age of planet Earth. It is approximately 4.5 billion years old. Rocks found in Canada have been carbon dated to be 3.96 billion years old and some in Australia to be over 4 billion years. It is calculated that it would have taken at least 400 million years for Earth to have developed enough hydrogen and oxygen to support simple life forms; another few million years to become habitable for human life. This would still mean that Earth was capable of supporting human life at least a couple of billion years before our traditional view that it all began only 6 million years ago. There is a huge reservoir of scientific studies available to those who want to dig into all the details to support the conclusions of science. There are also many articles that have been written to present the alternate view of "creationists". It tends to be wrapped up in a theory referred to as "theistic evolution". It is not my intention here to attempt to go through all that information. I want to keep it as simple as I can for my readers. What I will be presenting is the conclusions I have come to and why. If that does not satisfy my reader, I would say you have the opportunity to go through that same process yourself.

I believe there was intelligent life in existence on Earth before the Garden of Eden narrative of the Bible. I, also, believe that if my Evangelical friends continue to insist that the Bible must be correct in every detail, that is an argument they are ultimately going to lose. Does that mean, then, I must abandon the Biblical narrative and declare it invalid. Absolutely not! I will be arguing to the contrary later in this chapter. You are going to need to look at the history of the Bible and the section on God's activity in the world to understand why I have come to the conclusions I have.

THE HISTORY OF THE BIBLE

The Bible is the most important historical document in the history of the world. How it came to be is something that needs to be studied and understood. When we truly do that we will stand in awe in trying to understand how it survived at all. Yet, it has become the pillar upon which Western Civilization has built its culture, its system of jurisprudence, and its system of ethics and social justice.

There is still a significant number of folks out there who hold to the simplistic view that the Bible was simply handed down one day by a Deity that wanted to inform the world of His will. Others believe that early scribes along with Moses wrote at least the first five chapters. In my conclusions here, I will be relying heavily on the work done by William Schneidewind, who holds the Kershaw Chair of Ancient Eastern Mediterranean Studies at UCLA. His work has been ground breaking in helping us understand this great mystery.

The first thing you must understand is that for hundreds of years there was no written language. Writing was non-existent. Israel was a pastoral and agrarian society and the people totally illiterate. All of the stories had to be passed on by what we refer to as an "oral tradition". It must be assumed that there were some more capable of memorization than others and they would have been chosen to tell the stories. This is not a process that occurred in one life time. It was something that lasted for hundreds of years and perhaps longer. It is not until about the 10th century B.C. that we begin to see evidence of early writing. A tablet discovered at an excavation in Tel Zayit, Israel in 2005 is one of the earliest.

As writing came into existence, it was something reserved only for the elite and the priests. Writing was considered magical. There were no books as we think of them today. Writing had to be done on clay tablets or on hides or bits of papyrus. Little by little the "oral tradition" began to be written down, one little piece at a time. But, the magic of writing was still confined to the Temple and the Palace. In order for a religious document to have any authority with an entire people, they must be literate and have access to the information. That did not begin to occur until about the 8th century B.C. with the rise of the Assyrian Empire. They had introduced a process of Urbanization and Globalization in order to strengthen their hold on their territories. This included writing so that merchants and soldiers and the common man had access. This became important in Ancient Palestine where writing became important for an increasingly complex society. This process continues through the 6th Century B.C. Ultimately it was the development of the Hebrew language, and the ability to pull all of the biblical information together that turned Israel from a society that relied on "oral tradition" and listening to the teacher into a society that was textualized. With textualization came an almost automatic sense of authority. The Word could now be read from a text. It was the democratization in Ancient Palestine that allowed the scriptures to gain the acceptance and religious authority in the book we now call the Bible.

This did not occur without some difficulty. There were groups that had a vested interest in keeping the authority of the "oral tradition" and the prophetic word. There were also challenges because of the years of exile in Babylonia. Babylonia had conquered the Assyrians in the north and had made slaves out of most of Israel. Most recent studies indicate that Israel was depopulated by as much as 80% during the exile. During that time, the Royalty of Israel was given access to the southern palace of Babylonia. There they continued their writing of Biblical literature and they collected literature from the royal and temple library. By the end of the exile, the core of the Hebrew text of the Bible was complete. The struggle, however, between those who preferred the authority of the "oral tradition" and those who wanted the written word continues all the way up to the destruction of the Temple in 70 A.D. by the Romans. After that, Christians quickly adopted the Codex, the forerunner to the modern book. Codixes with bound leaves begin to appear in the First Century A.D. It was the technological development of the codex that first gave the Bible its physical form.

Later on we begin to see entire books of the Bible written by a single author within one lifetime. That was not true in the Old Testament. Perhaps one of most important elements in this development was the rapid expansion of the Greek language. This became the language of choice for much of the New Testament writing. The wide dissemination of the Bible does not occur until the development of the printing press by Gutenberg and his first printing of the Bible in 1454 A.D. Before this time, you would have had to be very wealthy to possess even one of the Biblical manuscripts. They were like gold. With the advent of printing, the Biblical manuscripts became more available to the masses. But, now there was an additional problem. Which of the hundreds of Biblical manuscripts were divinely inspired?

The process of canonization of the Old Testament is a history unto itself. My readers need to understand that what we call the Old Testament is for the most part the traditional Hebrew Bible. However, large sections of it are not included in the Jewish Bible. When Martin Luther did his translation of the Bible he also excluded those books that had been traditionally excluded by the Jews. He grouped them together in a separate group he called the Apocrypha. When this process was carried out in development of the New Testament canon, the later books were added to Luther's and we have a separate volume of Biblical manuscripts called the Apocryphal Books. That book is available for those that want to dig further into that history. It includes ones like "The Gospel according to Mary".

Someone had to decide which of these manuscripts deserved to be included in the Bible. For the Catholic Church, most of those decisions were made at the Council of Trent in 1546 A.D. For the Protestants that continues all the way to the Westminster Confession of Faith in 1657. For a long time, the New Testament

Canon did not include some of the books that are now there. For example, it did not include Hebrews, or II Peter, James or Jude or I John and II John. The very last book to be accepted into the Canon was Revelation which did not occur till the very end of the process.

Perhaps this brief overview of how the Bible came to be will help my readers understand the almost magical reality of how it survived at all. Certainly, if you are a logical and thinking person, you could not look at all that history and still insist that there could not be one error any place along the line. Despite that, I will continue to argue for the authority of the Bible and will be giving you my reasons.

HOW GOD HAS REVEALED HIMSELF TO MAN

In order to have a full understanding or even a somewhat superficial understanding of this question would require several years of study and perhaps several lifetimes. There are thousands of scholarly works that are available to the true student. But, let's face the reality of the world in which we live. The average professing Christian not only has a very limited knowledge of the Bible, but most have no working knowledge of the Holy Spirit or of its importance in the everyday life of a "born again" Christian. When I set about to do this book, it was my clear intention to attempt to cut through the scholarly maze with its thousands of citations and present a cogent outline that the average layman could follow to find his or her way to the Father. The need to find our way to God is a universal yearning even though we don't always want to hear what that means. It is my desire to help facilitate that process.

There are three different and distinct ways that God has revealed Himself to man. All three of those ways have been empowered by the Holy Spirit. Let's look at each of them:

1.   REVELATION: This is a process initiated by the Holy Spirit where the active will of God is made known in revealed

knowledge that would have been beyond the recipient's ability to know. Perhaps the best example of this is the handing down of the Ten Commandments to Moses. That revelation alone has become the cornerstone of Western Civilization. There are hundreds of other examples throughout scripture.

2. MIRACLES: Most of God's activity in the world is accomplished through natural law. However, there have been events down through Biblical history as well as in more recent times that cannot be explained by natural law. We have come to refer to those as miracles. They are evidence of the fact that God is, indeed, God, and can when necessary intervene against His own created natural law. Let me give you a couple of examples that will clarify this issue for you. When the Holy Spirit whispered to the Virgin Mary that she was with child, Mary had known no man. The Immaculate Conception was, in fact, a miracle. On the other hand, when Hannah became pregnant with Isaac in the Old Testament, the scripture says that Abraham knew Hannah, a clear implication of a sexual contact between them. The resulting birth was accomplished through natural law.

3. DIVINE PROVIDENCE: That leads me to number three, Divine Providence. This is the most common of the ways that God reveals himself. The English word providence comes from the Latin providencia. It literally means "foresight". It is through Divine Providence that God has inserted Himself into history. For example, you see evidence of God's hand when you read the entire story of Joseph. God's people are in captivity in Egypt. Joseph is forced by his jealous brothers into slavery with an Egyptian caravan. Joseph, however, ends up is a position of high authority in Egypt and becomes a significant part of the release of the captives by the Pharaoh upon the return of

Moses. Here is an example of Divine Foresight in order to bring about the result God obviously wanted. Divine Providence may be something that occurs very quickly or it can be something that might take centuries. We may not recognize it till after the fact. However, it is always accomplished through natural law.

I believe this is the appropriate place to bring up a point I have been wanting to make. It is clear, when you look at the historical record, that God chose the Hebrew people to be the vehicle for nurturing His Word and for the ultimate coming of His Son Jesus. Why He chose them, I don't know. He could have chosen any group of people or any culture, but He chose the Hebrews. We see the working of Divine Providence over the centuries as enemies of the Hebrew people were destroyed to preserve God's prophetic Word. We are talking about the third leg of the Godhead. God, the Father, God, the Son, and God, the Holy Spirit. Three distinct entities, Deities all, and yet one complete entity. This is the mystery of the Trinity. It is a concept that is still being grappled with by theologians.

Let's go back now to our discussion of the Old Testament. I will begin by stating with no reservation that I believe the Bible to be the inspired and revealed Word of God. Now, you are going to ask, how can I square that with what I said before? Let me explain.

Remember what God was dealing with back at the beginning. He had chosen the Hebrew people to be the instrument that would be used to ultimately bring His Son into the world. That would have to be accomplished over centuries and with an illiterate and primitive people. If you are a good parent and you are trying to teach your young children, what do you do? Especially, if they have no reading or writing skills? You teach them with simple stories and parables and metaphors. Then as they grow older and more mature you add more substance to their information. It is my contention that the Bible was the vehicle that God needed for that point in

History. It remains a cherished treasure and will continue to be so for the next million years.

Now God's children have grown up. We now have knowledge that the primitive peoples could not have even imagined. We now have an understanding of our universe that makes it possible for us to gain greater insight into the birth of our planet as well as what lies beyond in the vast expanses of space. I said that what God accomplished with the Bible had been done by Divine Providence and the leading of the Holy Spirit. I firmly believe that. Let's take a minute to look more closely at the Holy Spirit. References to the Holy Spirit occur over 90 times in the Bible. However there are only two references to being led by the Spirit. Both occasions are by Paul, the Apostle. The first is Galatians 5/18 "If you are led by the Spirit, you are not under the law." The second is Romans 8/14 "For those who are led by the Spirit of God are the Children of God." You need to go back and read both the fifth chapter of Galatians and the eighth chapter of Romans to get a clear understanding of the working of the Spirit.

It is clear to me that God used the leading of the Spirit to bring his children from ignorance toward maturity. There is no earthly way the Bible could have survived all those centuries but for the hand of the Holy Spirit. But, are we to assume that once the Bible was canonized into its present form, all at once, God ceased to speak to us through the Spirit? I think not. The questions we need to be asking are not, should we abandon the faith of our fathers and continue our arguments with the science community? The question we need to ask and should be strongly focused on is: What is God's message for us today? How are we to use this new knowledge to discover God's will for the next generation? If we truly have become adults, then we must face up to that challenge.

UNDERSTANDING THE POWER AND PURPOSE OF THE BIBLICAL NARRATIVE

I have said that God was using the Bible narrative to lead his children with the use of stories. But those stories had power and purpose. What answers were the Hebrew children seeking? Who am I? Where did I come from? Is there a God? Why is there evil in the world? The biblical narrative gives answers to all of those questions. First there is the creation. Never mind if it was 7 days or 15 billion years, God created it. This is followed by the Garden of Eden episode. That story makes clear that man had free will. He had a choice. Without free will there can be no sin, and without sin there would be no need for redemption. The entire episode with the tempting of Eve by the serpent and her leading Adam to follow her lead is a powerful and compelling story. It is not one that would be easily forgotten by God's Hebrew children. It would be carried as part of the "oral tradition" through the centuries.

The explanation for the existence of evil is equally compelling. It is explained with the introduction of Lucifer. Without Lucifer, theologians would be forced to conclude that God Himself created Satan. But why would an all good God create a monster like Satan? Lucifer bails us out. God created a beautiful and angelic Chief of Angels in Lucifer. He is given power in heaven; but, Lucifer, just like Eve and Adam has free will. He had a right to make a choice, and he chooses to attempt to make himself the Godhead. He is cast out of heaven and given a Hell over which he can rule. You can go back to the account of the fall of Lucifer in Isaiah 14 and Ezekiel 28.

There are many explanations for evil in the world. Some fall in the natural world. Many bad things result from natural disasters and what we refer to as culpable and non-culpable ignorance. But after all of those explanations are exhausted, there is still an evil spirit that haunts the Earth. Jesus clearly defines him as Satan. Him I believe. Whether he was a pre-existent entity at the time of creation or the result of the fall of Lucifer, he is a source for evil in the world.

As a seminarian, I always found it easier to try to explain the existence of evil, then to try to understand the existence of good. We all have sinned and fallen short, so we can relate to the temptations of moral impropriety or the sins of greed, and avarice. But, unless you put God and the working of the Holy Spirit into the equation, good becomes very difficult to explain. You are ultimately forced to conclude that the source of good in the world is God. We are taught by scripture that God created us in His own image. He has placed a Spirit within us that can be Godlike. When we are in tune with the Father and being "led by the Spirit" we are extensions of God on Earth. That same Spirit, however, can be ruled by Satan. It is always our choice.

As the Hebrew children continue to grow and mature, more is revealed to them. The entire Old Testament is really a history of a people. It leads us through the Prophetic books, two exiles, many times when God's chosen people could have been destroyed, but were not. It becomes crystal clear in retrospect that this entire process is being used to set the stage for the coming of Jesus. Yes, the Bible is the inspired Word of God, and presenting it as He did, it served God's purpose for that time in history. However, the Bible is not the final word or an end unto itself. God is still speaking and only He has the final word.

HOW DIVINE PROVIDENCE HAS INFLUENCED MY LIFE

When I was twelve years old, I gave my life to Christ. This is a commitment I made again on a moonlit hill at Camp Comeca in Cozad, Nebraska. It is a commitment that has never changed throughout my life. There have been many times when I have fallen short and had to get on my knees to get right with God but, I have never ceased to try to be "led by the Spirit". That has been true whether I was doing secular work, or my preferred work as God's spokesman. In return, I can point to dozens of times that I think Divine Providence gave me the edge I needed. If you have read my story carefully, you can identify those occasions yourself. Divine Providence could also have been in play with some of the things that did not happen. You can look at that and judge for yourself. The bottom line is, God brought me to a place to end my career as it began, as His spokesman. No blessing could be greater. My life has come full circle, I have found my way to the Father.

14

Finding Your Way to the Father

IT IS MY FERVENT HOPE THAT THIS STORY WILL HELP you to find your way back to the Father if you have lost your way. If you are in a good place with your faith and have the assurance that comes from being right with God, then God bless you. Yet, the reality remains that thousands, even within the community of faith, have lost their way and need a way back home. Let's talk a bit about that journey.

There are many traditional ways that we use to seek a closer walk with God. Certainly, reading and study of the Bible is important. Quiet times for prayer and reflection are necessary for restoking the power of the Spirit. Surrounding ourselves with others who seek to follow the Faith is helpful. But, what if you have lost your way? My answer to you is going to be so simple that it would not take a rocket scientist to figure it out. But, just because it is simple does not mean it is not profound.

Do you remember in Sunday School, we all saw the artist's rendering of the Good Shepherd? Jesus is standing and cradling a little lamb on His breast. The scripture associated with that picture is the story Jesus gives us of the Good Shepherd. The Good

Shepherd, a metaphor for God, "leaves the ninety and nine and seeks the one that is lost". God is the Good Shepherd, and He never gives up seeking those who are seeking Him. If you are that one, know that right now God is knocking on your door. You have the option to ignore His call, or you can with full contrition and humble adoration answer His call. Offer up this prayer: Father I have sinned. I am deeply sorry for my failures and seek your forgiveness for all my shortcomings. If that prayer is sincere and genuine, and you do intend to walk, henceforth, by "the leading of the Spirit, there will never, ever, be a refusal. The Good Shepherd will have found the one that was lost. You will find your way back to the Father. It sounds so simple, and it is. But it is the overriding message of the Gospel.

May God's blessing be upon you as you make your journey back to God and to a renewal of your faith. May it conclude with the assurance that you have found your way back to the Father. Amen.

Printed in the United States
By Bookmasters